More praise for *The Emotional Lives of Animals* and Marc Bekoff

"In clear and convincing language, Marc Bekoff provides rational defense for what many of us already sense — that animals can feel sorrow, joy, anger, and pleasure much as we humans do. Bekoff proves that this idea not only is compatible with the fact of evolution but is required by it. Once science considers the argument of this finely reasoned book, it will never be the same."

— David Rothenberg, professor of philosophy, New Jersey Institute of Technology, and author of *Why Birds Sing* and *Sudden Music*

"A thought-provoking, compassionate, and scholarly work from one of the world's most eminent behavioral scientists."

— Ian Dunbar, founder of the Association of Pet Dog Trainers and author of *Before & After Getting Your Puppy*

"Move over, Darwin. And prepare to be moved. In *The Emotional Lives of Animals*, world-class scientist Marc Bekoff argues forcefully that our emotions are the gifts of our animal ancestors. Bekoff's new book itself is a gift that invites us to explore and appreciate the passionate lives of animals. Weaving the latest scientific data about empathic mice and elephants suffering from PTSD with wonderful stories about laughing dogs and pissy baboons, Bekoff's forward-looking book offers both an explanation and an ethical compass that points the way toward hope for the ways in which we interact with other animals."

— Marty Becker, DVM, resident veterinarian on *Good Morning America* and author of *The Healing Power of Pets*

"Marc Bekoff is one of those rare scientists who can talk real sense about animals because he is aware of being an animal himself. Read this wonderful book."

— Mary Midgley, author of *Animals and Why They Matter* and *The Ethical Primate*

"*The Emotional Lives of Animals* is not a tearjerker but a gritty portrait of individual and societal values, painted with a heady blend of soul and science. But Bekoff's refreshing candor and solid credibility make it a must-read for all."

— *City Dog*

"A passionate, thoughtful book."

— *BBC Wildlife*

"This is a book that will empower and give hope; it guides the reader not into a pit of despair over the cruelties humans inflict on other animals but into a light, helping us seek the way forward."

— Captive Animal Protective Society, UK

"[Bekoff] presents both touching anecdotes and scientific evidence to support his case that animals do indeed have feelings — rich emotional lives, in fact."

— *Dog Fancy*

"As a boy studying Buddhism in Tibet, I was taught the importance of a caring attitude toward others. Such a practice of nonviolence applies to all sentient beings — any living thing that has a mind. Where there is a mind, there are feelings such as pain, pleasure, and joy. No sentient beings want pain; instead, all want happiness. Since we all share these feelings at some basic level, as rational human beings we have an obligation to contribute in whatever way we can to the happiness of other species and try our best to relieve their fears and sufferings. I firmly believe that the more we care for the happiness of others, the greater our own sense of well-being becomes. Therefore, I welcome Marc Bekoff's book *The Emotional Lives of Animals*."

— His Holiness the Dalai Lama

"An extraordinary, intelligent, and valuable book about a subject one might be forgiven for thinking taboo since it is so absent from discussion: an exploration of the other animals' feelings, the emotional makeup we share with them yet often do not know exists, forget entirely, deliberately ignore, or casually disregard. Here we see animals, whole and complete, thinking their not-so-private thoughts, grieving, loving, jumping for joy, and fleeing that which is painful or upsetting. And it makes us think about who they are and what our impact is and can be on their lives. Marc Bekoff not only captures poignant incidents of the animals' emotions as evidenced by observations and pure common sense but brings to each discovery his own vital repertoire of human emotion and expression. A glorious, moving, important book to enjoy and share."

— Ingrid Newkirk, cofounder and president of
People for the Ethical Treatment of Animals (PETA)

The Emotional Lives of Animals

ALSO BY MARC BEKOFF

Animal Passions and Beastly Virtues: Reflections on Redecorating Nature

Animals Matter: A Biologist Explains Why We Should Treat Animals with Compassion and Respect

Minding Animals: Awareness, Emotions, and Heart

Nature's Life Lessons: Everyday Truths from Nature (with Jim Carrier)

Species of Mind: The Philosophy and Biology of Cognitive Ethology (with Colin Allen)

Strolling with Our Kin (a children's book)

The Ten Trusts: What We Must Do to Care for the Animals We Love (with Jane Goodall)

Wild Justice: Reflections on Empathy, Fair Play, and Morality in Animals (with Jessica Pierce; forthcoming in 2009)

EDITED BY MARC BEKOFF

Animal Play: Evolutionary, Comparative, and Ecological Perspectives (with John Byers)

The Cognitive Animal: Empirical and Theoretical Perspectives on Animal Cognition (with Colin Allen and Gordon Burghardt)

Coyotes: Biology, Behavior, and Management

Encyclopedia of Animal Behavior

Encyclopedia of Animal Rights and Animal Welfare

Encyclopedia of Human-Animal Relationships: A Global Exploration of Our Connections with Animals

Listening to Cougar (with Cara Blessley Lowe)

Readings in Animal Cognition (with Dale Jamieson)

The Smile of a Dolphin: Remarkable Accounts of Animal Emotions

The Emotional Lives of Animals

A Leading Scientist Explores Animal Joy, Sorrow, and Empathy — and Why They Matter

MARC BEKOFF

FOREWORD BY JANE GOODALL

New World Library
Novato, California

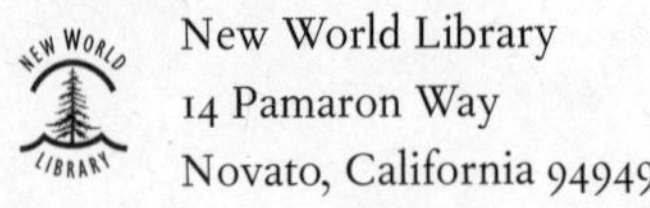

New World Library
14 Pamaron Way
Novato, California 94949

Text design and typography by Tona Pearce Myers

Photograph of Marc Bekoff and Pablo, a rescued hybrid Podenco-Galgo mix from Spain, by Johanna Esser.

Cover photograph of Kamots and Motomo copyright © 2002 by Jim and Jamie Dutcher (www.livingwithwolves.org). Kamots is the gray alpha male and Motomo is the black mid-ranking male showing submission and respect by licking Kamots's face, which also reinforces bonds of solidarity among pack members.

Library of Congress Cataloging-in-Publication Data
Bekoff, Marc.
The emotional lives of animals : a leading scientist explores animal joy, sorrow, and empathy, and why they matter / Marc Bekoff ; foreword by Jane Goodall.
p. cm.
Includes bibliographical references and index.
ISBN 978-1-57731-502-5 (hardcover : alk. paper)
1. Emotions in animals. I. Title.
QL785.27.B45 2007
591.5—dc22 2006038278

First paperback printing, June 2008
ISBN: 978-1-57731-629-9
Printed in the USA on 100% postconsumer-waste recycled paper

g New World Library is a proud member of the Green Press Initiative.

10 9 8

For Jasper, the spokes-bear for hope and freedom,
and Pablo, chimpanzee CH-377,
two among far too many

Contents

Foreword

I am very pleased to be writing a foreword for this important book, for it deals with a subject — animal emotions — that is crucial to a proper understanding of animals and their relationship to ourselves. Throughout my childhood I was fascinated with animals of all sorts — I watched them, learned from them, and loved them. At the age of ten I developed a very special relationship with an extraordinarily intelligent mixed-breed dog, Rusty, who became my constant companion. He, along with the three successive cats, two guinea pigs, one golden hamster, one canary, and two tortoises with whom we shared our house and our hearts, taught me that animals, at least those with reasonably complex brains, have vivid and distinct personalities, minds capable of some kind of rational thought, and above all, feelings.

And then, in 1960, I had the extraordinary opportunity to learn about the chimpanzees of the Gombe National Park in Tanzania. Knowing nothing of scientific method, I simply recorded everything I saw. It was fortunate that I was patient, for during the first few months they fled whenever they saw the strange white ape who had appeared so suddenly in their midst. The first individual to lose his fear I named David Greybeard. He was a strikingly handsome adult male, with large eyes set far apart. With his gentle but determined personality he was, as I ultimately discovered, a real leader. David's calm acceptance of my presence helped other members of his community to realize that I was not, after all, such a frightening creature. Then, many of them became aggressive, treating me to the kind of intimidation displays normally directed at leopards or large snakes. But eventually they relaxed, and as I gradually gained their trust, they allowed me to move into their world — always on their terms. I got to know the various vivid personalities: David's close companion Goliath, who was, as I eventually realized, the alpha male; high-ranking, assertive Flo and her large family; timid Olly with her far-from-timid daughter, Gilka; irritable JB; Jomeo, the inadvertent clown — and all the rest.

After a year Louis Leakey arranged for me to go to Cambridge University to work toward a PhD in ethology. There I was criticized for my lack of scientific method, for naming the chimpanzees rather than assigning each a number, for "giving" them personalities, and for maintaining they had minds and emotions. For these, I was told sternly, were attributes reserved for the human animal. I was even reprimanded for referring to a male chimpanzee as "he" and a female "she": Didn't I know that "it" was the correct way to refer to an animal? Well, a *nonhuman* animal. And so, for the most part, my observations were written off as merely those of a naive young woman who had had no university education. Yet it had been that very *lack of qualifications*, along with my passion for learning about animals in the wild, that had appealed to my mentor, the late Louis S. B. Leakey. He wanted an observer whose mind was unbiased by what he felt was the reductionist thinking of scientists in the early sixties. Indeed, ethologists, along with many philosophers and theologians, argued that personality, mind, and emotions were uniquely human attributes and that the behavior of other-than-human animals was for the most part merely a response to some environmental or social stimulus.

But I could not accept this — it absolutely contradicted all I had learned during my years with Rusty and my new experiences with the chimpanzees. Fortunately, I had a wise thesis supervisor, Professor Robert Hinde. He himself was known for his rigorous scientific mind and his intolerance of fuzzy thinking. Yet he had named all the rhesus monkeys he was studying and wrote of them, unashamedly, as he's and she's. It was Robert Hinde who taught me to express my common sense but ethologically revolutionary ideas in a way that would protect me from too much hostile scientific criticism. For example, I could not say, "Fifi was happy," since I could not *prove* this: but I could say, "Fifi behaved in such a way that, had she been human, we would say she was happy"!

During the late sixties, more and more biologists went into the field and started long-term studies on all manner of animal species: apes, monkeys, elephants, whales, dolphins, wolves, and so on. And these studies made it clear that animal behavior is far more complex than was originally admitted by Western science. There was increasingly compelling evidence that we are not alone in the universe, not the only creatures with minds capable of solving problems, capable of love and hate, joy and sorrow, fear and despair. Certainly we are not the only animals who experience pain and suffering. In other words, there is no sharp line between the human animal and the rest of the animal kingdom. It is a blurred line, and becoming more so all the time.

Yet unfortunately, there are countless people among both the scientific and lay communities who still genuinely believe that animals are just objects, activated by responses to environmental stimuli. And only too often these people, consciously or unconsciously, reject our attempts to persuade them otherwise. After all, it is easier to do unpleasant things to unfeeling objects — to subject them to painful experiments, raise them in intensive factory farms, and hunt, trap, eat, and otherwise exploit them — than it is to do these things to sapient, sentient beings. Fear in a monkey, a dog, or a pig being is probably experienced in much the same way as it is in a human being. Young animals, human or otherwise, show such similar behavior when they are well fed and secure — frisking, gamboling, pirouetting, bouncing, somersaulting — that it is hard not to believe they are not expressing very similar feelings. They are, in other words, full of *joie de vivre* — they are happy. I have watched chimpanzee children, after the death of their mothers, show behavior similar to clinical depression in grieving human children — hunched posture, rocking, dull staring eyes, lack of interest in events around them. If human children can suffer from grief, so too can chimpanzee children. Sometimes, in this state of grieving, chimpanzee orphans — like Flint and Kristal — die.

It is becoming increasingly obvious, and there is now excellent scientific backing to support this, that animals can be very therapeutic, very healing. They play an important role in decreasing high blood pressure, reducing antisocial behavior in prisoners, and helping children with learning disabilities to read. Elderly people, living alone, can be saved from depression caused by loneliness, or feelings of uselessness, when they share their lives with a beloved cat or dog. This is not just because animals are soft, furry, and warm. It is because these animal healers seem to empathize with their humans, understand their needs — and love them. These animals, in other words, are a great deal more than objects whose behavior is triggered by stimulus and response. A mechanical stuffed toy animal, no matter how skillfully crafted, no matter how lifelike it appears, will never take the place of a living, feeling, and loving animal.

The more people understand that animals, especially group-living mammals with complex brains, have rich emotional lives and, above all, are capable of suffering — mentally as well as physically — the sooner we may succeed in changing the inappropriate ways in which so many millions of animals are treated. In fact, most people have no idea what goes on in medical research labs. And they do not know — and do not want to know — about the billions of animals raised in stinking, unsanitary, and unbelievably cramped spaces in factory farms. Nor do they understand the cruelty involved in training animals to perform for circuses and other forms of entertainment. Unfortunately, so long as some scientists continue to uphold (at least in their professional lives) the mistaken view that other-than-human beings are mere *things*, this will be used to condone inhumane behavior of this sort.

That is why I am so glad that Marc has written this book. Undaunted by the sometimes vicious criticism from his peers that has been leveled at him throughout most of his professional life, he has continued to study and write about the personalities and emotions of other-than-human animals. And now in *The Emotional Lives of Animals* he has pulled together the growing body of scientific evidence that supports the existence of a variety of emotions in other animals, richly illustrated by his own careful observations and conclusions. He argues forcefully that the time has come for acceptance of this body of information across the board. He suggests, in fact, that it is a waste of time even to ask if chimpanzees, elephants, dogs, and so on experience happiness, sadness, despair, and anger — that this is self-evident to anyone who has spent time or shared his or her life in a meaningful way with animals. Instead of continuing to try to *prove* the obvious, surely the time has come to *accept* that animal beings, like human beings, express emotions, and to ask different questions — as he does in this book. Why did emotions evolve in the first place? What useful purpose do they serve?

The Emotional Lives of Animals adds a strong voice to the growing chorus of those who are trying to change attitudes toward the animal beings with whom we share this planet. Combining careful scientific methodology with intuition and common sense, this book will be a great tool for those who are struggling to improve the lives of animals in environments where, so often, there is an almost total lack of understanding. I only hope it will persuade many people to reconsider the way they treat animals in the future.

— Jane Goodall, PhD, DBE,
founder, the Jane Goodall Institute,
and United Nations Messenger of Peace

PREFACE

The Gift of Animal Emotions

Welcome to the fascinating world of animal emotions. As a scientist who's studied animal passions and beastly virtues for more than thirty years, I consider myself very fortunate. I love what I do. I love learning about animals, and I love sharing with others what my colleagues and I discover. Whenever I observe or work with animals, I get to contribute to science and develop social relationships at the same time, and to me, there's no conflict between those two activities.

Before I begin, however, I'd like to address an important matter of terminology. In discussions of "animal emotions," we sometimes forget that humans are also animals. However, it's cumbersome to use the phrase "nonhuman animals" to refer to beings we typically call "animals." And so in this book I use the word *animals* to mean "nonhuman animals" — realizing of course that we're all animals, and hopeful that this linguistic shorthand won't perpetuate any "forgetfulness."

The field of animal emotions — which is a specific area of focus within the larger scientific discipline of cognitive ethology, or the study of animal minds — has changed a great deal in the past thirty years. When I first began my studies, researchers were almost all skeptics who spent their time wondering if dogs, cats, chimpanzees, and other animals felt anything. Since feelings don't fit under a microscope, these scientists usually didn't find any — and as I like to say, I'm glad I wasn't their dog! But thankfully, there are fewer and fewer skeptics today, and while debates over *whether* animals have emotions still occur, the question of real importance is becoming *why* animal emotions have evolved the way they have. In fact, the paradigm is shifting to such an extent that the burden of proof now falls more often to those who still argue that animals don't experience emotions. My colleagues and I no longer have to put tentative quotes around such words as *happy* or *sad* when we write about an animal's inner life. If our dog, Fido, is observed to be angry or frightened, we can say so with the same certainty with which we discuss human emotions. Scientific journals and the popular press regularly publish stories and reports on joy in rats and grief in elephants, and no one blinks.

It's bad biology to argue against the existence of animal emotions. Scientific research in evolutionary biology, cognitive ethology, and social neuroscience supports the view that numerous and diverse animals have rich and deep emotional lives. Emotions have evolved as adaptations in numerous species, and they serve as a social glue to bond animals with one another. Emotions also catalyze and regulate a wide variety of social encounters among friends, lovers, and competitors, and they permit animals to protect themselves adaptively and flexibly using various behavior patterns in a wide variety of venues.

Charles Darwin's well-accepted ideas about evolutionary continuity, that differences among species are differences in degree rather than kind, argue strongly for the presence of animal emotions, empathy, and moral behavior. In practice, continuity allows us to "connect the evolutionary dots" among different species to highlight similarities in evolved traits, including individual feelings and passions. What we have since learned about animal emotions and empathy fits well with what we know about the lifestyles of different species — how complex their social interactions and social networks are. Emotions, empathy, and knowing right from wrong are keys to survival, without which animals — both human and nonhuman — would perish. That's how important they are.

And there are always surprises. Just when we think we've seen it all, new scientific data and stories appear that force us to rethink what we know and to revise our stereotypes. For example, just after receiving the galley proofs of this book, I came across a story in the December 2, 2006 issue of *New Scientist* magazine about emotions in whales. It turns out that humpback whales, fin whales, killer whales, and sperm whales possess spindle cells in the same area of their brains as spindle cells in human brains. This brain region is linked with social organization, empathy, intuition about the feelings of others, as well as rapid, gut reactions. Spindle cells, once thought to be unique to humans and other great apes, are believed to be important in processing emotions. And whales actually have more of them than humans do.

All mammals (including humans) share neuroanatomical structures and neurochemical pathways that are important for feelings, but do all animals feel the same things? Research has shown that mice are empathic rodents, but it turns out that they're fun-loving as well. We also will hear stories of pleasure-seeking iguanas, a horse with a sense of humor, amorous whales, elephants who suffer from psychological flashbacks and posttraumatic stress disorder, a grieving otter, a bereaved donkey, pissed-off baboons, sentient fish, and a sighted dog who served as a "seeing-eye dog" for his canine buddy.

While we might expect to find close, enduring, and endearing emotional relationships forming between members of the same species, improbable relationships often occur between animals of wildly different species, even between animals who are normally predator and prey! Such is the case with Aochan, a rat snake, who befriended a dwarf hamster named Gohan, at Tokyo's Mutsugoro Okoku Zoo.

If a snake and a hamster can become friends, then why not humans and other animals? Of course, they do all the time. But it's not just human emotions at play in these relationships; the emotions of animals attract us and bond us as well. During a series of lectures I gave at the Assistance Dog Institute in Santa Rosa, California, in August 2006, I was able to observe the interactions between people with a wide range of disabilities and the dogs who were their lifelines. As I watched the nuanced, nitty-gritty details of communication that occurred through voice and movements, each person and his or her dog displayed a strong reciprocal social bond that was clearly based on mutual respect and feeling. Both beings, human and canine, shared an enduring emotional attachment that went far beyond "mere training."

I often begin my lectures with the question: "Is there anyone in this audience who thinks that dogs don't have feelings — that they don't experience joy and sadness?" I've never had an enthusiastic response to this question, even in scientific gatherings, though on occasion a hand or two goes up slowly, usually halfway, as the person glances around to see if anyone is watching. But if I ask, "How many of you believe that dogs have feelings?" then almost every hand waves wildly and people smile and nod in vigorous agreement. To live with a dog is to know firsthand that animals have feelings. It's a no-brainer. We map their feelings by observing their behavior, guided by the analogy of our own emotional templates, and we do it very reliably. And today, I'm happy to say, even the majority of scientists agree with what seems like common sense to everyone else.

Recognizing that animals have emotions is important because animal feelings matter. Animals are sentient beings who experience the ups and downs of daily life, and we must respect this when we interact with them. Animals are not only the companions we live with, care for, and love, they are also the billions of other domesticated animals who live on farms and in slaughterhouses and provide us with food and clothing. And wild animals are continually faced with trying to share our ever-crowded world.

Our relationship with other animals is a complex, ambiguous, challenging, and frustrating affair, and we must continually reassess how we should interact with our nonhuman kin. Part of this reassessment involves asking difficult questions, and making sure our actions match our understandings and beliefs. Thus, I often ask researchers who conduct invasive work with animals or people who work on factory farms: "Would you do that to your dog?" Some are startled by this question, but it's a very important one to ask. If we wouldn't do something to our companion animals that we do daily to mice, rats, monkeys, pigs, cows, elephants, chimpanzees, or even noncompanion cats and dogs, we need to ask ourselves why.

Humans have enormous power to affect the world any way we choose. Daily, we silence sentience in innumerable animals. However, we also know that we're not the only sentient creatures with feelings, and with this knowledge comes the enormous responsibility and obligation to treat other beings with respect, appreciation, compassion, and love. There's no doubt whatsoever that, when it comes to what we can and cannot do to other animals, it's their emotions that should inform our discussions and our actions on their behalf, and we can always do more for them. This is a forward-looking book of hope that stresses that we must be imaginative in our interactions with other animals.

Emotions are the gifts of our ancestors. We have them and so do other animals. We must never forget this.

Acknowledgments

First, I thank all the wonderful animal beings I've been lucky enough to know in a wide variety of situations. More than thirty-five years ago, their willingness to share their lives and their passions with me was instrumental in my deciding that I wanted to come to terms with their emotions and their worldviews. Moses, Mishka, Inuk, Sasha, Jethro, Zeke, Maddy, Sukie, Willie, Scrap, Max, Toso, and other canine buddies have patiently listened to me talk about their feelings and made me a better dog.

Jan Nystrom, Jaak Panksepp, Jessica Pierce, Michael Tobias, and Nancy McLaughlin provided comments on various sections of this book. They, along with Colin Allen, Jonathan Balcombe, Iain Douglas-Hamilton, Michael W. Fox, Jane Goodall, Lori Gruen, Dale Jamieson, Mary Midgley, Cynthia Moss, Jill Robinson, and Sue Townsend have influenced my thinking about animal emotions and why they matter, and I've learned a lot from their wisdom. Jim McLaughlin alerted me to the notion of fish as "streams of dietary proteins."

Jill Robinson, Betsy Webb, Mim Rivas Eichler, Michael Tobias, CeAnn Lambert, Louis Dorfman, Scott Coleman, and Marty Becker shared stories that I've included here. Jim and Jamie Dutcher graciously provided the wonderful photograph for the cover. Their nonprofit organization, Living with Wolves (www.livingwithwolves.org), is dedicated to educational outreach and dispelling dangerous myths and misconceptions about wolves and other predators.

When Boniface Zakaria, my guide in Tanzania, spotted a tiny chameleon on a blade of grass while driving at fifteen miles an hour in the Serengeti National Park — a little speck I couldn't see until I was standing six inches from it — I fully realized how much keen observers of animal behavior can miss even when we're giving our full attention to what we're doing. Thank you, Boniface, for this humbling lesson.

At New World Library, Kristen Cashman was very helpful in organizing the final production of this book, and Monique Muhlenkamp graciously helped with publicity as I traveled the world in cars, planes, boats, and trains. Jeff Campbell did a wonderful job of copyediting, and my editor, Jason Gardner, was very patient and kind. He went far beyond the call of duty in cleaning up and reorganizing an early draft of this book before Jeff got his hands on it! It truly was a pleasure working with them.

CHAPTER 1

The Case for Animal Emotions and Why They Matter

Many animals display their feelings openly, publicly, for anyone to see. And when we pay attention, what we see outside tells us lots about what's happening inside an individual's head and heart. As we'll find, careful scientific research is validating what we intuitively understand: that animals feel, and their emotions are as important to them as ours are to us.

A few years ago my friend Rod and I were riding our bicycles around Boulder, Colorado, when we witnessed a very interesting encounter among five magpies. Magpies are corvids, a very intelligent family of birds. One magpie had obviously been hit by a car and was lying dead on the side of the road. The four other magpies were standing around him. One approached the corpse, gently pecked at it — just as an elephant noses the carcass of another elephant — and stepped back. Another magpie did the same thing. Next, one of the magpies flew off, brought back some grass, and laid it by the corpse. Another magpie did the same. Then, all four magpies stood vigil for a few seconds and one by one flew off.

Were these birds thinking about what they were doing? Were they showing magpie respect for their friend? Or were they merely acting *as if* they cared? Were they just animal automatons? I feel comfortable answering these questions, in order: yes, yes, no, no. Rod was astounded by how deliberate the birds were. He asked me if this was normal magpie behavior, and I told him that I'd never seen anything like this before and hadn't read any accounts of grieving magpies. We can't know what they were actually thinking or feeling, but reading their actions there's no reason not to believe these birds were saying a magpie farewell to their friend.

Despite the more than three decades I've spent studying animal species, I never cease learning from the individuals I encounter. Red foxes live near my mountain home outside of Boulder, Colorado. As I stare into the eyes of a red fox sitting by my study and watching me type, or as I observe red fox pups playing with one another or a female red fox burying her mate, I can't help but reflect deeply on what it's like to be these individuals sharing my hillside. Many animals live on the surrounding land — coyotes, mountain lions, porcupines, raccoons, black bears, a wide variety of birds, and lizards, along with many dogs and cats. Through the years, they've been my friends and teachers.

In my musings about animal emotions I also can't help wondering, What about the insects? Do even mosquitoes have emotional lives? Of course, mosquitoes have tiny brains and lack the neural apparatus necessary for the evolution of emotions, so it's doubtful they do. But in truth, we just don't know. One day, perhaps we'll figure out a way to determine this. More important, however, would it make a difference to us if they did? It should, just as it should make a difference to us that other animals have emotions. Knowing that animals feel — and being able to understand them when they express joy, grief, jealousy, and anger — allows us to connect with them and also to consider their points of view when we interact with them. Knowledge about animal passions should make a difference in how we view, represent, and treat our fellow beings.

THICK SKIN AND TENDER HEARTS:

Babyl the Elephant and Her Unconditional Friends

A recent trip to Kenya and Tanzania opened my eyes to the world of elephants, who are some of the most amazing beings I've ever seen. Observing large groups of wild elephants close up I could feel their majestic presence, awareness, and emotions. These firsthand experiences were wholly different than seeing captive elephants, who often live alone, in the confines and unnatural settings of a zoo, and my visit was deeply spiritual, inspirational, and transformative.

While we were watching a group of wild elephants living in the Samburu Reserve in Northern Kenya, we noted that one of them, Babyl, walked very slowly. We learned that she was crippled and that she couldn't travel as fast as the rest of the herd. However, we saw that the elephants in Babyl's group didn't leave her behind; they waited for her. When I asked our guide, the elephant expert Iain Douglas-Hamilton, about this, he said that these elephants always waited for Babyl, and they'd been doing so for years. They would walk for a while, then stop and look around to see where Babyl was. Depending on how she was doing, they'd either wait or proceed. Iain said the matriarch even fed her on occasion.

Why did the other elephants in the herd act this way? Babyl could do little for them, so there seemed no reason for or practical gain in helping her. The only obvious conclusion we could draw was that the other elephants cared for Babyl, and so they adjusted their behavior to allow her to remain with the group.

Friendship and empathy go a long way. And Babyl's friends aren't an isolated example. In October 2006 in a small village in eastern India, a group of fourteen elephants crashed through a village looking for a group member who had fallen into a ditch and drowned. Residents had already buried the seventeen-year-old female elephant, but still, thousands of people were forced to flee their homes as the other elephants searched and rampaged for more than three days.

THE HEART *IS* THE MATTER

In September 2006 there was a meeting about animal welfare called "The Heart of the Matter." It's nice to see scientists finally using the word *heart*, for the heart is the matter.

I study animal emotions and I love what I do. Over the course of my career, I've studied a wide variety of animals — coyotes, wolves, dogs, Adélie penguins, archer fish, western evening grosbeaks, and Steller's jays — and I've tackled a wide range of questions, dealing with everything from social behavior, social organization, and social development to communication, play, antipredatory behavior, aggression, parental behavior, and morality. To me, the evidence for animal emotions is impossible to deny, and it is widely supported by our current knowledge in animal behavior, neurobiology, and evolutionary biology.

In fact, the study of animal emotions is a dynamic and rapidly developing field of science, and there's no shortage of interest in animal emotions among scientists and average folks alike. In March 2005 about six hundred people from more than fifty nations gathered in London at a landmark meeting sponsored by the Compassion in World Farming Trust to learn more about animal sentience, animal consciousness, and the emotional lives of animals. In October 2006 the World Society for the Protection of Animals organized a conference in Rio de Janeiro to discuss how to improve animal welfare on farms and in research labs. Organizers expected about two hundred people, but twice that many attended, coming predominantly from Brazil and surrounding countries. The favorable response to the meetings in London and Rio is indicative that the time really has arrived for us to come to terms with the emotional lives of animals.

Stories about animal emotions and our complicated interrelationships with animals appear with increasing frequency in the press, from prestigious scientific journals like *Science*, *Nature*, *Trends in Ecology and Evolution*, and the *Proceedings of the National Academy of Sciences* to the *New York Times*, *Psychology Today*, *Scientific American*, *Time*, *The Economist*, and even *Reader's Digest*. The emotional lives of animals was even the subject of a surprise hit movie, *The March of the Penguins*. Released in summer 2005, the documentary poignantly depicts penguin feelings and demonstrates how they experience suffering but also how they endure the most extreme challenges as they care for their eggs and their young.

Nevertheless, despite mounting scientific evidence and widespread popular belief, a decreasing few within the scientific community remain skeptical. Some still doubt that animal emotions even exist, and many who believe they do exist tend to think animal emotions must be lesser than human ones. This seems to me an outdated and even irresponsible point of view, and my main goal in this chapter — and indeed throughout the book — is to show that animal emotions exist, that they are important to humans, and that this knowledge should influence how we treat our fellow animals.

In discussing animal emotions, I focus mainly on behavioral data and anecdotal stories, weaving in recent discoveries in social neuroscience to show how a combination of common sense and scientific data — what I call "science sense" — makes a strong case for the existence of beastly passions. While stories drive much of my discussion, I bring in scientific studies as necessary for support.

However, once we agree that animal emotions exist and that they matter — which is what a great many people already believe — then what? Then we must consider ethics. We must look to our actions and see if they are consistent with our knowledge and beliefs. I feel strongly that ethics should always inform science. We should always strive to merge knowledge, action, and compassion. Indeed, that is always the heart of the matter.

WHAT ARE EMOTIONS?

It is very difficult to answer the question, "What are emotions?" Most of us know emotions when we see them but find it difficult to define them. Are they physical, mental, or both? As a scientist, I feel safe saying that emotions are psychological phenomena that help in behavioral management and control; they are phenomena that emote us, that make us move. A distinction is often made between "emotional responses" to physical reactions and "feelings" that arise from thoughts. Emotional responses show that the body is responding to certain external stimuli. For example, we see an oncoming car about to hit us and we feel fear — increasing our heart rate, blood pressure, and body temperature. But actually, the fear isn't felt until the brain responds to the physiological changes that were a reaction to seeing the oncoming car.

Feelings, on the other hand, are psychological phenomena, events that happen solely in an individual's brain. An external event may trigger one emotion, such as anger or grief, but upon reflection we may decide we feel differently. We may interpret our emotions. Feelings express themselves as different moods. Feelings help us and influence how we interact with others in a wide variety of different social situations.

Charles Darwin, the first scientist to study animal emotions systematically, recognized six universal emotions: anger, happiness, sadness, disgust, fear, and surprise. He maintained these core emotions help us deal rapidly with a wide variety of circumstances and help us to get along in a complex social world. Others have since added to his list. Stuart Walton, in his book *A Natural History of Human Emotions*, adds jealousy, contempt, shame, and embarrassment to Darwin's core group, while the neuroscientist Antonio Damasio (in *Descartes' Error*) says that social emotions also include sympathy, guilt, pride, envy, admiration, and indignation. It's interesting that none of these researchers mention love.

Which, if any, of these emotions do animals experience? And do animals experience any emotions that humans do not? This is a very interesting question. Ethologist Joyce Poole, who has studied elephants for many years, states: "While I feel confident that elephants feel some emotions that we do not, and vice versa, I also believe that we experience many emotions in common."

If Poole is right, then there may be some emotions that animals experience that humans will never understand, but there are many that we do. Aren't animals, human and nonhuman alike, happy when playing or when reuniting with a loved one? Don't animals become sad after losing a close friend? When wolves reunite, wagging their tails loosely to and fro in a circle, whining and jumping about, are they not displaying happiness? What about elephants who reunite in a greeting celebration, flapping their ears and spinning about and emitting a vocalization known as a "greeting rumble" — is this not happiness? Likewise, what name but grief can we give to the emotion that animals display when they remove themselves from their social group, sulk after the death of a friend, stop eating, and even die? Surely, despite differences, all species must share a similar core of emotions.

PRIMARY AND SECONDARY EMOTIONS

Researchers usually recognize two different types of emotions, primary and secondary emotions. *Primary* emotions are considered to be basic inborn emotions. These include generalized rapid, reflex-like ("automatic," or hardwired) fear and fight-or-flight responses to stimuli that represent danger. They require no conscious thought and include Darwin's six universal emotions: fear, anger, disgust, surprise, sadness, and happiness. Animals can perform a primary fear response, such as avoiding an object, almost unconsciously, before they have even recognized the object generating the reaction. Loud raucous sounds, certain odors, objects flying overhead: these and other such stimuli are often inborn signals for "danger" that cause an automatic avoidance reaction. There's little or no room for error when confronted with a dangerous stimulus, so natural selection has resulted in innate reactions that are crucial to individual survival.

Primary emotions are wired into the brain's evolutionarily old limbic system (especially the amygdala); this is the "emotional" part of the brain (so named by Paul MacLean in 1952). The physical structures in the limbic system and similar emotional circuits are shared among many different species and provide a neural substrate for primary emotions. In his three-brains-in-one (or triune brain) theory, MacLean identifies the reptilian, or primitive, brain (possessed by fish, amphibians, reptiles, birds, and mammals); the limbic, or paleomammalian, brain (possessed by all mammals); and the neocortical, or "rational" neomammalian, brain (possessed by a few mammals, such as primates and humans) — all packaged into the cranium. Each is connected to the other two, but each also has its own capacities. While the limbic system seems to be the main area of the brain in which many emotions reside, current research now indicates that not all emotions are necessarily packaged into a single system, and there may be more than one emotional system in the brain.

Secondary emotions are more complex emotions, and they involve higher brain centers in the cerebral cortex. They could involve core emotions of fear and anger, or they could be more nuanced, involving such things as regret, longing, or jealousy. Secondary emotions are not automatic: they are processed in the brain, and the individual thinks about them and considers what to do about them — what action is the best one to perform in a certain situation. Conscious thought and secondary emotions can influence how we respond to situations that bring forth primary emotions: We may duck as an unseen object flies overhead, but as we recognize that it's only a shadow, we will refrain from running and instead, feeling a twinge of embarrassment, quickly straighten up and pretend nothing is wrong.

Thinking about the emotion allows for *flexibility* of response in changing situations after evaluating which of a variety of actions would be the most appropriate to perform in the specific situation. Sometimes, if someone is bothering you, it might be appropriate to get away from them, and sometimes this might create an even worse social situation — depending on who the person is and what kind of consequences you fear. Although most emotional responses are unconsciously generated —

they occur without thinking — we learn to try to think before acting. Thinking allows us to make connections between feelings and actions, and this allows for variability and flexibility in our behavior so that, depending on the social situation, we always do the right thing. In this way, evidence of emotions in any creature is also an important step in determining sentience and self-awareness.

DOGS ARE HAPPY, NOT "HAPPY"

> *The reason a dog has so many friends is that he wags his tail instead of his tongue.*
> — ANONYMOUS

We've all seen it. Maddy and Mickey, two of my friend's dogs, regularly have playdates at my house when their human companions are away. They arrive bounding around wildly in play, panting and barking, their wagging tails seemingly propelling them through space. They try to play with anyone who's available, whirling around to catch their own tail, running amok and knocking down anything and anyone in their way, stopping only for a taunting pause and then jumping into play once again. There's no question about it: these dogs are having fun!

For most people, spending half an hour with a dog is all the "proof" they need that animals have emotions, for dogs don't hide what they feel. The Nobel Prize–winning ethologist Konrad Lorenz gave us a very simple and common example when he noted how publicly emotional dogs are when they're anticipating going on a walk. Lorenz wrote in *Man Meets Dog*: "The owner says without special intonation and avoiding mention of the dog's name, 'I don't know whether I'll take him or not.' At once the dog is on the spot, wagging his tail and dancing with excitement.... Should his master say, 'I don't think I'll take him, after all,' the expectantly pricked ears will drop sadly.... On the final pronouncement, 'I'll leave him at home,' the dog turns dejectedly away and lies down again."

Thankfully, the dismissively skeptical line that animals only act "as if" they're feeling joy, grief, anger, or pain is now essentially dead. I know no practicing researcher who doesn't attribute emotions to their companion animals — who doesn't freely anthropomorphize — at home or at cocktail parties, regardless of what they do at work. (This anthropomorphizing is nothing to be ashamed of, by the way; as Alexandra Horowitz and I have argued, and as I show in chapter 5, these scientists are simply doing what comes naturally. Anthropomorphizing is an evolved perceptual strategy; we've been shaped by natural selection to view animals in this way.) Indeed, behavioral and neurobiological studies have consistently shown, and it is now largely accepted as fact, that animals share the primary emotions, those instinctual reactions to the world we call fear, anger, surprise, sadness, disgust, and joy.

Scientists now agree on the universality of the primary emotions based on studies that show that humans and animals share similar chemical and neurobiological systems. For instance, animals are frequently used to develop and to test drugs for human use in mental disorders, and a recent study shows that mice can be a good model for sadness and introversion. After mice are bullied or consistently dominated by other mice, they become withdrawn, and these depressed mice respond to such human drugs as the antidepressant Prozac. In another example, suicidal rats — or rats who have toxoplasmosis and develop a suicidal attraction to cats — can be successfully treated with antipsychotic drugs. When given haloperidol, which is used to control schizophrenia, their fondness for cats decreases greatly. The veterinarian Nicholas Dodman suggests using similar drugs along with behavioral conditioning for problem dogs and cats. If animals respond to these drugs as humans do, then it's highly likely that they have similar neural underpinnings to their emotions and probably similar feelings.

Scientific data and numerous stories indicate that animals feel a wealth of secondary emotions as well. Many people already know this simply through everyday observation of their pets. Science has been slower to accept this "common wisdom," but that's perhaps to be expected; one important function of science is to "objectively" validate direct, subjective experience.

Empathy or compassion is an important secondary emotion to identify in animals, for it demonstrates a selfless caring for others. Recall Babyl and her caring friends. While I was in Homer, Alaska, I read a similar story about two grizzly bear cubs who stuck together after they were orphaned when their mother was shot near the Russian River. The female cub remained with her wounded sibling, though he limped, swam very slowly, and needed help to get food. An observer noted, "She came out and got a fish, and pulled it back, and then she let the other one eat." The young female obviously cared for her brother, and her support was crucial for his survival.

There's also a story of a troop of about a hundred rhesus monkeys in Tezpur, India, that brought traffic to a halt after a baby monkey was hit by a car. The monkeys encircled the injured infant, whose hind legs were crushed and who lay in the road unable to move, and blocked all traffic. A government official reported that the monkeys were angry, and a local shopkeeper said: "It was very emotional. . . . Some of them massaged its legs. Finally, they left the scene carrying the injured baby with them."

In one classic study, a hungry rhesus monkey would not take food if doing so subjected another monkey to an electric shock, and there is a more recent scientific study on empathy in mice. In this study, either one or both members of a pair of adult mice were injected with acetic acid, causing them to writhe in pain, so that researchers could observe whether or not these rodents have the capacity to feel for others who are in pain. Researchers discovered that mice who watch their peers in pain are more sensitive to it themselves and that an injected mouse writhed more if its partner was also writhing. Mice used visual cues to generate the empathic response, although they typically use scent in many of their social encounters. So, as we see in the stories that open this chapter, animals (including mice) possess empathy. In addition, it's also known that the empathic response in mice is mediated by the same brain mechanisms as in human empathy.

Of course, this study is troubling. Did the scientists need to cause such pain to reach their conclusions? Mice (and rats) currently aren't protected by the Animal Welfare Act, but perhaps these and other findings will be used to elevate their status to that of dogs, cats, and nonhuman primates when it comes to invasive experimental testing. As we see in chapter 6, the Animal Welfare Act is far from an adequate protection in itself, but it would be a start.

After this scientific study of empathy appeared, I received numerous stories about empathy in a wide variety of animals, including rodents. People who live with animals weren't surprised by the findings. CeAnn Lambert, who runs the Indiana Coyote Rescue Center, told me that one hot summer morning she saw two baby mice in a deep sink in her garage. They were trying to get out of the sink but couldn't get up the steep, slick sides. One seemed less exhausted than the other. CeAnn put some water in a lid and placed it in the sink, and immediately the more lively pup went over to get a drink. On the way to the water the mouse found a piece of food and picked it up and took it over to its littermate. The weak mouse tried to take a bite of the food while the other kept moving the food slowly toward the water. Finally, the weaker mouse got a drink. Both gained some strength and climbed out using a board that CeAnn put in the sink.

There are many more examples, but the point is that even if animal emotions aren't exactly the same as our own, or for that matter the same across species, this doesn't mean that animals don't feel. In fact, as these last stories indicate, animal emotions are not restricted to "instinctual responses," but entail what seems to be a good deal of conscious thought.

IF ANIMALS FEEL, THEN WHAT DO THEY KNOW?

Animals Have Their Secrets But Their Feelings Are Transparent

The reluctance of contemporary philosophers and scientists to embrace the view that animals have minds is primarily a fact about their philosophy and science rather than a fact about animals.

— DALE JAMIESON,
"SCIENCE, KNOWLEDGE, AND ANIMAL MINDS"

When animals bark, howl, purr, whimper, grunt, laugh, or squeal, it means something to them, and what they're saying should also mean something to us, for their feelings matter. Lynne Sharp points out in her wonderful book *Creatures Like Us?* that the interests and concerns of animals are as important to them as ours are to us. Tails talk to us about what animals are feeling, and so too do various postures, gaits, facial expressions, sounds, and odors. Sometimes I wish I had a tail and mobile ears so I could communicate more effectively with dogs and other animals, whose tails and ears tell us lots about what they're thinking and feeling. Wagging wildly or drooping between their legs, animals' tails allow us to enter into their own brand of sentience.

What animals know — and how much self-awareness they have — is a topic of wide and often heated debate. The growing scientific evidence is that they know quite a lot, but the difficulties of communicating across species may make it impossible to ever know exactly how much. My baseline concerning animal emotions and sentience is pretty simple — animals will always have their secrets, but their emotional experiences are transparent. In other words, we know that numerous animals feel a rich panoply of emotions, some of which, like empathy, require a certain level of conscious thought. Many animals display a sense of humor. A few animals, such as chimpanzees, dolphins, and elephants, have passed tests that demonstrate they possess self-awareness. Some might experience a sense of awe, and some might even be moral beings who know "right" from "wrong."

Of course, there are differences among species. We would expect variations based on social, ecological, and physical factors. However, there also are compelling similarities despite sometimes extreme differences. One common measuring stick is called "relative brain size" (brain size expressed as a ratio to body size), and indeed, just about all researchers agree that, when comparing species, relative brain size makes a difference in various aspects of behavior, including antipredatory and feeding strategies. Just what these types of differences mean, however, remains largely a mystery, but there's no evidence that it means that animals with a smaller ratio don't have rich emotional lives. Because we share old parts of the brain that are important in human emotions, namely the limbic system including the almond-shaped structure called the amygdala, focusing solely on relative brain size is misleading. We need to pay attention to what we share with other animals and not necessarily how much of it we share with them. The brains of mice, dogs, elephants, and humans differ greatly in size, but all of these species display joy and empathy.

Unfortunately, misconceptions continue, often in popular books that offer unsupported generalizations about the cognitive, emotional, and empathic capacities of animals. For example, Harvard psychologist Daniel Gilbert, in his popular bestseller *Stumbling on Happiness* claims that "*The human animal is the only animal that thinks about the future*" (Gilbert's italics) and that this "is a defining feature of our humanity." Not even the animal emotion skeptics I know would ever make this claim; there are literally volumes of data showing that individuals of many species do think about the future, from Mexican jays, red foxes, and wolves caching food for later retrieval, to a subordinate chimpanzee or wolf pretending that she doesn't see a favored food item in the presence of a dominant individual and later returning to eat it when the dominant animal isn't around. We're also told by Gerald Hüther in his book *The Compassionate Brain* that the capacity for empathy sets the human brain apart from all other nervous systems, despite scientific evidence that this just isn't so.

In the end, the truth is simply that a dog has rich emotional and cognitive experiences of the *dog kind*. Ethological studies and research in social neuroscience show that humans aren't the sole occupants of the emotional arena. Dogs and many other animals can be happy, sad, and get pissed off. They let their tails do the talking. Animals talk to us using a myriad of behavior patterns — postures, gestures, and gaits — along with their mouths, tails, eyes, ears, and noses.

ANIMALS AND HUMANS:
Sharing Emotions, Sharing Lives

Animal emotions are a matter of importance in their own right, but the very presence of animals — with their free-flowing emotions and empathy — is also critical to human well-being. Animal emotions should be important to us because we need animals in our lives; they help us. It's because animals have emotions that we're so drawn to them; lacking a shared language, emotions are perhaps our most effective means of cross-species communication. We can share our emotions, we can understand the language of feelings, and that's why we form deep and enduring social bonds with many other beings. Emotions are the glue that binds. They catalyze and regulate social interactions in animals and in humans.

Veterinarian Marty Becker's book *The Healing Power of Pets* showed how pets can keep people healthy and happy — they help to heal lonely people in nursing homes, hospitals, and schools. In *Kindred Spirits*, holistic veterinarian Allen Schoen points to fourteen concrete ways in which a relationship between animal companions and humans has been shown to reduce stress. These include reducing blood pressure, increasing self-esteem in children and adolescents, increasing the survival rate of heart attack victims, improving the life of senior citizens, aiding in the development of humane attitudes in children, providing a sense of emotional stability for foster children, reducing the demand for physician's services for nonserious problems among Medicare enrollees, and reducing loneliness in preadolescents. And Michelle Rivera, in her book *Hospice Hounds*, tells numerous stories of how dogs and cats can help people who are near death.

A recent study showed that a visit from a friendly pup might be good medicine for an ailing heart. In a randomized study of seventy-six hospitalized heart-failure patients, UCLA researchers found that anxiety scores dropped an average of 24 percent among patients who interacted with canines, regardless of the breed. The dogs would lie on the patients' beds for twelve minutes while patients simply patted and scratched their ears. "This study demonstrates that even a short-term exposure to dogs has beneficial physiological and psychosocial effects on patients who want it," said Kathie Cole, a clinical nurse at the UCLA Medical Center.

Similarly, in my home state, inmates at the Colorado Women's Correctional Facility get to care for and live with dogs who would have been put to sleep at the local animal shelter. The experience of walking the dogs, grooming them, and cleaning up after them is incredibly rewarding and beneficial to everyone — the inmates, the dogs, and the prison staff.

Stories of wild animal and human encounters — and other cross-species relationships — echo the conclusions of these studies. Lions are magnificent carnivores and powerful predators, yet they also show compassion, sympathy, and empathy in very unpredictable ways. For example, three lions in Ethiopia rescued a twelve-year-old girl from a gang who had kidnapped her. Said Sergeant Wondimu Wedajo: "They stood guard until we found her and then they just left her like a gift and went back into the forest." Stuart Williams, a wildlife expert with the country's rural development ministry, said that it was likely that the young girl was saved because she was crying from the trauma of her attack. Williams said, "A young girl whimpering could be mistaken for the mewing sound from a lion cub, which in turn could explain why [the lions] didn't eat her. Otherwise they probably would have done so." Eventually, three of the four kidnappers were caught.

In but one of many stories of dolphins helping humans at sea, in New Zealand, a pod of dolphins circled protectively around a group of swimmers to fend off an attack by a great white shark. "They started to herd us up. They pushed all four of us together by doing tight circles around us," said Rob Howes, one of the swimmers. In these stories, we see that the empathetic presence of animals can have a direct and immediate impact on our well-being and even survival.

If it seems strange that animals would go out of their way to care for us, that's not even half the story. Some of the relationships that animals form are unbelievably improbable — for instance, in the Samburu Reserve in northern Kenya, a lioness adopted a baby oryx, usually a lion's favored meal, on five different occasions. And at Tokyo's Mutsugoro Okoku Zoo, a rat snake named Aochan befriended a dwarf hamster named Gohan. The hamster was originally offered as a meal; Aochan had refused to eat frozen mice, and zookeepers figured that the hamster would be more appetizing. However, Aochan refused to eat the animal and seemed to prefer sharing a cage with her; now Gohan even naps on Aochan's back. Even though Aochan has begun eating frozen rodents, he still shows no interest in eating his friend. Kazuya Yamamoto, a keeper at the zoo, said, "Aochan seems to enjoy Gohan's company very much."

And what do we make of the following fish story? Mary and Dan Heath claim that their adult golden retriever, Chino, is best friends with a fifteen-inch koi named Falstaff. For the past six years, the pair meets regularly at the edge of the pond where Falstaff lives. Each day, when Chino arrives, Falstaff swims to the surface and greets him and nibbles on Chino's paws. As Falstaff does this, Chino stares down with a curious and puzzled look on her face. Their close friendship is extraordinary and charming — as well as a powerful demonstration of just how important contact with other beings really is.

I have many personal stories that illustrate this as well, and I'll share two that involve my longtime canine companion, Jethro. One day, when Jethro was about two years old, after playing in the yard, he ran to the front door and waited to be let in. As he sat there, I noticed a small furry object in his mouth. My first reaction was, "Oh no, he killed a bird." But when I opened the door, Jethro dropped a very young, very alive bunny at my feet — drenched in his saliva. I couldn't see any injuries, but I decided to keep the bunny until I was sure it would be able to survive on its own. I named her Bunny, and I guessed that Bunny's mother had disappeared, probably eaten by a coyote, red fox, or mountain lion. Jethro looked up at me, wide-eyed, clearly seeking praise for being such a good friend to the bunny. This I gave him with a pat on his head and a rub of his tummy.

As I gathered a box, blanket, and food for Bunny, Jethro got very agitated. He tried to snatch her from my hands, and he whined and followed me around, watching my every move. When I had to leave the box, I called Jethro to come, but he wouldn't leave. I thought he'd try to snatch Bunny or the food, but he never did; he just stood watching for hours on end, fascinated by this little ball of fur slowly trying to get oriented in her new home. Jethro even slept next to Bunny, and during the two weeks I nursed her back to health, Jethro didn't harm her once. Indeed, Jethro had adopted Bunny, and all his attention was focused on making sure no one harmed her. Even when the day came to return Bunny to the outdoors, so she could begin life as a full-fledged rabbit, Jethro simply watched as she cautiously sniffed around, then slowly hopped away.

Nine years after this, Jethro again came running up to me with a wet animal in his mouth. Hmm, I wondered, another bunny? This time the wet ball was a young bird who was stunned from flying into a window. I held it in my hands for a few minutes till it regained its senses, and Jethro, true to form, watched every move. When I thought it was ready to fly, I placed the bird on the porch railing. Jethro approached it, sniffed, stepped back, and watched it fly away.

Jethro loved other animals, and he saved two from death. He could easily have eaten each with little effort. But you don't do that to friends.

When animals express their feelings they pour out like water from a spout. Animals' emotions are raw, unfiltered, and uncontrolled. Their joy is the purest and most contagious of joys and their grief the deepest and most devastating. Their passions bring us to our knees in delight and sorrow. If animals didn't show their feelings, it's unlikely that people would bond with them. We form close relationships with our pets not only because of our own emotional needs but also because of our recognition of theirs. As a resident of the Rocky Mountain foothills, I love rocky landscapes and rivers and streams, but I don't feel as close to them as I do to animal beings. I believe this is because landscapes and bodies of water don't have feelings or a point of view — they're not sentient.

Shared emotions and their gluelike power to attract and bind are responsible for this country's billion-dollar pet industry. More than 60 percent of U.S. households have a least one companion animal, and more than 55 percent have a dog or a cat. But the variety of animals kept as pets, particularly worldwide, is astonishing; it includes rodents, birds, fish, amphibians, reptiles, insects, spiders, invertebrates, and many more. About 20 percent of U.S. households have a bird, and more than 600 million pet fish are sold each year. In the both the United States and Britain, the numbers of pets are growing.

A Special Relationship: Children and Animals

I work with children as part of Jane Goodall's Roots & Shoots program, whose purpose it is to stimulate children to develop respect for animals, people, and the environment. This isn't difficult: children are curious naturalists who easily bond with all sorts of creatures. Children also provide some of the best examples of the powerful effect of animal emotions and empathy on human lives. More than 75 percent of children in the United States live with pets, and children are more likely to grow up with a pet than with both parents. American boys are more likely to care for pets than for older relatives or younger siblings. A vast majority of children refer to their pets as "family" or "special friends" and confidants, and more than 80 percent refer to themselves as their pet's mother or father. If stranded on a desert island, more than half of children would prefer the company of their pet rather than of family members. Children also worry about homeless pets.

A study of 394 U.S. university students showed that those who had lived with dogs or cats as children were more self-confident than those who did not. In a study conducted in Croatia, children who lived with dogs were more empathic and pro-socially oriented than children who did not live with dogs, and children with a greater attachment to their pets rated their family climate significantly better than children who were less attached. Interactions with pets also help children learn that their pets have needs different from their own and foster the development of a children's theory of mind (their pets have their own beliefs and view of the world).

Pets can be social catalysts and help to draw out autistic and socially withdrawn children (an increase in pro-social behaviors). The term "pet therapy" was coined by Boris Levinson more than four decades ago, and it is still in use today. An American child psychologist, Levinson found that many children who were withdrawn and uncommunicative would come out and interact positively if his dog, Jingles, joined them in therapy sessions.

Pets also help victims of abuse by teaching them about unconditional love and buffering and overcoming trauma. In one study, pets were rated as more supportive than humans for sexually abused children. Pets provide support for children who have to overcome divorce or the illness or loss of a family member or close friend.

The value of animals to humans cannot be overstated. And it's their emotions that draw us to them. And yet, while we need animals, many animals would surely do much better without us.

A PARADIGM SHIFT:

Rethinking Our Assumptions and Revising Our Stereotypes

Questions about animal emotions and why they matter can generate a lot of heat. Our relationship with animals is complex, and how we treat animals often changes dramatically depending on the context. Many people can show tremendous love and devotion to animals who are their pets, but then, with little forethought, concern, or regret, they may go on to abuse animals in different settings in egregious ways. This is particularly true of scientists and the animals they keep at home and in the lab. My response to scientists (and others) who say they love animals and then, directly or indirectly, subject them to intentional pain and suffering is to say that I'm glad they don't love me! Unfortunately for animals, the relationship with humans has been, and remains, strongly asymmetrical. Human interests almost always trump animal interests.

A few years ago while reading the prestigious journal *Science*, I came across the following sentence: "More than any other species, we are the beneficiaries and victims of a wealth of emotional experience." The scientist who wrote this, Professor R. J. Dolan, cannot possibly know that this is true. Indeed, other animals might actually experience more vivid emotions than we do, both positive and negative. This sort of "humanocentrism" is what plagues the study of animal emotions, and it's also a large reason why animals are treated by such varying standards. Why are we so special? Why are we such deeply feeling animals, whereas other animals aren't? Looking at the state of the world today, I find it difficult to accept that we should be the standard against which other animals should be compared.

It's my hope that the study of human-animal interactions will put an end to useless dualisms such as "we" versus "them," the "laboratory" (where animals are often disposable objects) versus "the home" (where animals are highly valued friends), and "higher" animals versus "lower." These dualisms aren't accurate, and they surely do not foster the development and maintenance of deep, respectful, and symmetrical interrelationships between humans and other animals.

What I hope to foster is a paradigm shift in how we think about animals, how we study animal emotions and animal sentience, and what we do with the information we already have, "scientific" and otherwise. This paradigm shift involves revising our stereotypes about what the emotional lives of animals of different species are "supposed" to be like. Rather than presuming that fish feel less than mice and that mice feel less than chimpanzees, or that rats aren't as emotional as dogs or wolves, or in general that animals feel less (and know less and suffer less) than humans, let's assume that numerous animals *do* experience rich emotions and *do* suffer all sorts of pain, perhaps even to a greater degree than humans.

Such an assumption increasingly reflects the evidence. At the Rio conference I mention earlier, world-renowned scientist Ian Duncan pronounced with no hesitation that based on his and his students' research (along with that of other scientists), fish experience pain and fear. They're also cunning, deceitful, and display cultural traditions. Further, Donald Broom, a professor at Cambridge University in England, suggested the possibility that animals with more complex brains might deal more effectively with pain than animals with less complex brains because the former have more varied responses, more flexible behavior, to cope with aversive situations. Broom's intriguing hypothesis is that perhaps fish cannot deal with pain as effectively as animals with more complex brains, and because of this fish actually suffer more. When deciding what and how much animals feel, it's best to keep an open mind.

As I've said, when it comes to the sometimes unconscious double standard that people frequently have in the treatment of animals, I find the question "Would you do it to your dog?" to be a great leveler. If you wouldn't do something to your dog, why would you do it to any other being?

This paradigm shift would also change how we do science — it would create revisions in methods and changes of heart. The burden of proof would permanently shift to the side of the skeptics, who would have to "prove" their claims that animals don't experience emotions and don't really feel pain. It would no longer be acceptable to say that "since we really don't know what animals feel, let's assume whatever they feel, if anything, doesn't matter." This would change how scientists conduct experiments and tests, creating a more humane environment for everyone. Respecting, protecting, and loving animals wouldn't compromise science, nor would it mean we'd respect, protect, and love humans less. Does feeding your dog mean starving your children? No, with a little consideration and forethought, everyone can be cared for.

Most important, assuming that animals do experience rich emotions will never cause any harm. A lovely, unidentified quotation captures this well: "If I assume that animals have subjective feelings of pain, fear, hunger, and the like, and if I am mistaken in doing so, no harm will have been done; but if I assume the contrary, when in fact animals do have such feelings, then I open the way to unlimited cruelties.... Animals must have the benefit of the doubt, if indeed there be any doubt."

WHAT WE DO WITH WHAT WE KNOW

As a scientist, I'm often criticized for being antiscience because of my strongly pro-animal views. I'm not antiscience. It is in the best traditions of science to ask questions about ethics; it is not antiscience to question what we do when we interact with other animals. Ethics can enrich our views of other animals, as they are in their own worlds and as we relate to them in ours; they help us to see that their lives are worthy of respect, admiration, and appreciation. Indeed, it is out of respect, admiration, and appreciation that many humans seek out the company of whales, dolphins, polar bears, and birds.

We need animals in our lives just as we need air to breathe. We live in a wounded world in which many of us are alienated from animals and all sorts of nature. Animals are our consummate companions who help us each and every day. Without close and reciprocal relationships with other animal beings, we're alienated from the rich, diverse, and magnificent world in which we live. That's why we seek out animals for emotional support. Our old Paleolithic brains pull us back to what's natural but missing in our fast-moving world: close interrelationships with other beings that help us figure out who we are in the grand scheme of things. Animals comfort us and put us in touch with what really matters — other sentient beings. A sentient animal is one for whom feelings matter, as my colleague John Webster puts it.

If we can learn to live consistently from this perspective, it would change for the better a great many ways in which animals are used and abused by human society. In fact, we owe it to them to help them however, whenever, and wherever we can. We can begin by examining our own lives and making the best and most ethical choices possible. Through the clothes we wear and the food we eat, are we supporting humane industries and practices? If we see people we know making hurtful choices, can we help alert or educate them to change? Are there ways we can better educate ourselves and pursue more stringent animal protection legislation? Far too many animals are harmed each and every day worldwide. If we can change minds and hearts and especially current practices, we will make progress and there is hope.

In my own field, I know that solid science can easily be done with ethics and compassion. There's nothing wrong with compassionate or sentimental science or scientists. Studies of animal thought, emotions, and self-awareness, as well as behavioral ecology and conservation biology, can all be compassionate as well as scientifically rigorous. Science and the ethical treatment of animals aren't incompatible. We can do solid science with an open mind and a big heart.

I encourage everyone to go where their hearts take them, with love, not fear. If we all travel this road, the world will be a better place for all beings. Kinder and more humane choices will be made when we let our hearts lead the way. Compassion begets compassion and caring for and loving animals spills over into compassion and caring for humans. The umbrella of compassion is very important to share freely and widely.

JASPER AND PABLO:

Two Among Many

> *Every man and living creature has the sacred right to the gladness of spring.*
> — LEO TOLSTOY

I've dedicated this book to Jasper and Pablo. Jasper is a moon bear who was formerly kept in a crush cage on a bear bile farm in China. Crush cages are used to compress a bear's body to maximize the amount of bile the animal produces (which is extracted by means of a catheter inserted in the gall bladder). Jasper was kept in a tiny cage — a "rusting prison of torture," according to Jill Robinson, the founder of Animals Asia — and tortured repeatedly over the course of many years for his bile, a chemical used in traditional Chinese medicine. "This poor bear had been pressed down by a 'crush' which had reduced the height of the cage by half and had flattened Jasper to the floor," Robinson wrote to me. "Unable to sit or stand or hardly move, it is beyond belief to comprehend that this wild, intelligent bear lay there in this state for fifteen years before being rescued. Jasper was the victim of catheter implantation and his physical and mental agony must have been intolerable. A mischievous, fun-loving bear today, Jasper is everybody's friend, bears and people alike. His beautiful, trusting eyes show the absolute forgiveness of his species, and reinforces our goal of rescuing as many individual bears as possible."

In 2004, John Capitanio, associate director at a major primate research center, was asked if animals had emotions, and he dismissively responded that animals are "a neutral palette on which we paint our needs, feelings, and view of the world." Jasper is anything but a neutral palette. He's a deeply feeling being, not a thing, who was tortured repeatedly, and of

Jasper in the crush cage in which he was imprisoned for fifteen years. (Photo courtesy of Annie Mather/Animals Asia.)

A rehabilitated Jasper today. (Photo courtesy of Annie Mather/Animals Asia.)

course he didn't like it. How can any human being treat another feeling being this way? I like to call Jasper the "spokes-bear for hope and freedom." Despite his torture, Jasper forgave.

Pablo was a captive and mistreated chimpanzee, who was known as CH-377 in the New York University lab where he was kept. Using numbers rather than names is one way researchers distance themselves from the animals they exploit. Pablo's sad story was told in *Discover* magazine: "According to his research dossier, Pablo... had been darted 220 times, once accidentally in the lip. He had been subjected to 28 liver, two bone marrow, and two lymph node biopsies. His body was injected four times with test vaccines, one of them known to be a hepatitis vaccine. In 1993 he was injected with 10,000 times the lethal dose of HIV. The barrel-chested chimp had shrugged off AIDS and kept hepatitis at bay only to die of an infection aggravated by years of darts, needles, and biopsies."

Gloria Grow, who was with Pablo when he died, let the other chimpanzees see Pablo and observed: "Alone or in pairs, they tug at his arms, open his eyes, groom him, rub his swollen belly.... Before long the chimps wander off hooting. The hoots blossom into screams, and soon the walls of the chimp house echo with the sound of knuckles pounding steel." That spring Jane Goodall took some of Pablo's ashes with her to Tanzania "to sprinkle in the forests of Gombe, where chimps dance to stop the rain."

There are many thousands of animals to whom this book could be dedicated. Jasper and Pablo are two among far too many animals — billions a year — who are abused. The ways in which they and others are treated are an insult not only to them but also to us, for we are certainly beings who know right from wrong.

What animals feel is more important than what they know. IQs don't matter. It's worth recalling the utilitarian philosopher Jeremy Bentham's well-known statement concerning animal suffering: "The question is not, Can they *reason*? nor, Can they *talk*? but, Can they *suffer*?" For Bentham, it really didn't much matter if animals could think or if they were smart. Rather, Bentham was concerned with whether or not animals could suffer. Intelligence and suffering are not necessarily correlated, and clever animals don't suffer more than less clever individuals. Some skeptics argue that some animals might not have a well-developed sense of self. We'll see this isn't really the case, but even if animals don't know who they are, they can still suffer, they can still be aware of their feelings, and they can still clearly tell us and other animals what they want and what they don't want.

It's time to journey into the minds and hearts of animals and discover what they feel and why. When we deny that animals have feelings, it demeans both them and us. We can make their lives better with little effort other than accepting them for who they are and welcoming them into our world. We should do no less.

CHAPTER 2

Cognitive Ethology: Studying Animal Minds and Hearts

What we believe Equus asinus *most prefers is simply to be left alone so that they may graze casually, marvel at their surroundings, meditate on other life forms, drink plenty of water, have fun, sing, sleep, make love, raise their young, have parties and discuss the great issues of life.* — MICHAEL TOBIAS AND JANE MORRISON, *DONKEY*

What's a purring cat thinking or feeling? What's running through a dog's mind as she's running and playing? What's happening in an elephant's brain and heart as he nuzzles a dead mate? What's a donkey feeling as she quietly grazes and takes in her surroundings? I decided to become a cognitive ethologist because I want to know what swims around in the minds and hearts of other animals. To do this, I've had to learn how to listen to "tail talk" and how to properly distinguish between a howl, a whimper, and a squeal.

This chapter explains the field of cognitive ethology — what it is, how it developed, and what it tries to do — and it ends with an evocative taste of what ethological fieldwork entails. This brief excursion is all preparation for meeting animals up close and personal in the next chapter.

COGNITIVE ETHOLOGY:

Definitions and Goals

Cognitive ethology is the comparative, evolutionary, and ecological study of animal minds. It focuses on how animals think and what they feel, and this includes their emotions, beliefs, reasoning, information processing, consciousness, and self-awareness. Cognitive ethologists are interested in several things: they hope to trace mental continuity among different species; they want to discover how and why intellectual skills and emotions evolve; and they want to unlock the worlds of the animals themselves. Cognitive ethologists prefer to study animals in their natural environment — or in conditions that are as close as possible to their natural environment.

Interest in the emotional and mental capacities of animals has been around a long time, but the modern era of cognitive ethology, with its concentration on the evolution and evolutionary continuity of animal cognition, began with the appearance of Donald R. Griffin's 1976 book *The Question of Animal Awareness: Evolutionary Continuity of Mental Experience*. Griffin is often called "the father of cognitive ethology" and his major concern was to learn more about animal consciousness. He, too, wanted to come to terms with the difficult question of what it is like to be a particular animal.

Cognitive ethology attracts a lot of attention from researchers in many different fields, including those interested in animal well-being and animal protection. I see cognitive ethology as the unifying science for understanding the subjective, emotional, empathic, and moral lives of animals. However, when it comes to some of the challenging and exciting "big questions" that cognitive ethology raises (such as the evolution of social morality, which I address in chapter 4), the final answers require a cross-disciplinary approach. We need ethologists, geneticists, evolutionary biologists, neurobiologists, psychologists, anthropologists, philosophers, theologians, religious scholars, and religious leaders all to rise to the extremely difficult task of understanding animals' emotional and moral lives and figuring out how they compare to — and have played a role in the evolution of — human moral, ethical, and spiritual understandings.

Before we get there, however, we need to agree on some basic questions, such as, "How do we know animals feel or think anything?" We do know this, and one reason is because of behavioral flexibility. Animals display flexibility in their behavior patterns, and this shows that they are conscious and passionate and not merely "programmed" by genetic instinct to do "this" in one situation and "that" in another situation. For example, monkeys will choose not to engage in an experiment if they think they'll fail. Research has shown that rats often take a moment to reflect on what they've learned when running a maze; they pause and play back the route in their heads in reverse order and edit their experiences. When animals need to make decisions that involve selectively attending to specific stimuli and purposefully choosing among alternative actions, many are quite able to do so — they're aware of their surroundings and intentionally make appropriate, purposeful, and flexible choices in a wide variety of situations.

Flexibility in behavior is one of the litmus tests for consciousness, for a mind at work. Consciousness evolved because it allowed individuals to make choices when confronted with varying and unpredictable situations. However, once we've established that other animals have conscious minds, then we get to the really interesting questions. What are they thinking about? What do they feel? What do they know? The excitement to answer these questions is what drives cognitive ethologists. It's what gets us out of bed in the wee hours of the morning.

CHARLES DARWIN:
Evolutionist with a Heart

Charles Darwin is often credited with being the first scientist to give serious attention to the study of emotions. James Rachels paraphrases

Darwin as noting that mammals "experience (to greater or lesser degrees) anxiety, grief, dejection, despair, joy, love, 'tender feelings,' devotion, ill-temper, sulkiness, determination, hatred, anger, disdain, contempt, disgust, guilt, pride, helplessness, patience, surprise, astonishment, fear, horror, shame, shyness, and modesty." In his attempts to answer questions concerning the origin of emotional expression, he also appears to be the first person to apply the comparative method to the study of behavior. The comparative method refers to the study of closely related and more distantly related species to learn about similarities and differences in their behavior. Darwin used six methods to study emotional expression. These were 1) observations of infants; 2) observations of the insane who, when compared to normal adults, were less able to hide their emotions; 3) judgments of facial expressions created by electrical stimulation of facial muscles; 4) analyses of paintings and sculptures; 5) cross-cultural comparisons of expressions and gestures, especially of people distant from Europeans; and 6) observations of animal expressions, especially those of domestic dogs.

In *The Expression of the Emotions in Man and Animals*, Darwin wrote about his dog with great insight: "I formerly possessed a large dog, who, like every other dog, was much pleased to go out walking. He showed his pleasure by trotting gravely before me with high steps, head much raised, moderately erected ears, and tail carried aloft but not stiffly." When Darwin would change his walking route and the dog was unsure of whether his walk would continue, "His look of dejection was known to every member of the family.... This consisted of the head drooping much, the whole body sinking a little and remaining motionless; the ears and tail falling suddenly down, but the tail was by no means wagged .... His aspect was that of piteous, hopeless dejection."

Darwin argued that emotions evolved in both animals and humans for the purpose of furthering social bonds in group-living animals. He believed that emotions connected us with the rest of our community and with the rest of the earth. Furthermore, Darwin used observations of behavior such as pausing before solving problems to support his claim that even animals without language are able to reason.

In his careful research, Darwin repeatedly stressed that the differences among many species were differences in degree rather than kind. He argued that variations in mental abilities, for example, were differences along a continuum. So according to Darwin, there is evolutionary continuity among animals not only in anatomical structures such as hearts, kidneys, and teeth, but also in brains and their associated cognitive and emotional capacities.

In other words, if we look hard enough, we can find the roots of our own intelligence and emotions in other animals. Again, this doesn't mean that humans and other animals are identical, but rather that they share enough common physical or functional traits that their capacities fall on a continuum. That's what "evolutionary continuity" refers to: the similarities and contrasts among species are nuances or shades of gray, not stark black-and-white differences.

Darwin didn't hedge in his arguments about evolutionary continuity. "There is no fundamental difference between man and the higher animals in their mental faculties," Darwin wrote. He attributed cognitive states to many animals on the basis of observation rather than controlled experiments. In addition to making a strong case for mental continuity between humans and animals, Darwin also attributed feelings and emotions to nonhumans. For example, he claimed, "The lower animals, like man, manifestly feel pleasure and pain, happiness, and misery." Darwin also observed that monkeys were capable of deceit. About the first orangutan he saw at the London Zoo, he wrote he could see its passion and rage, sulkiness, and the very actions of despair. He observed that chimpanzees sulk and pout like children who feel disappointment, and that a rhinoceros at the zoo was "kicking and rearing out of joy."

As we'll see in more detail later, current cutting-edge research agrees with Darwin's observations and ideas. We now know that dogs and other animals share with humans some of the same brain structures and some of the same neurochemicals that form the basis for such emotions as joy. This process of identifying the evolutionary continuity of emotions is essentially the same as for purely physical attributes. We know that there are two-, three-, and four-chambered organs we call hearts because they pump blood. Just because the heart of a frog doesn't look like the heart of an eagle or of a human doesn't mean that a frog doesn't have a heart. Similarly, just because dog-joy and chimpanzee-joy and human-joy aren't exactly the same doesn't mean that any of these animals don't experience joy.

CURIOUS NATURALISTS

Dutch ethologist Niko Tinbergen, often called "the curious naturalist," has provided ethologists with a framework for studying animal behavior, and his suggestions are very helpful to researchers interested in cognitive ethology. In 1973, Tinbergen, Konrad Lorenz, and Karl von Frisch won the Nobel Prize in Physiology or Medicine for their pioneering work in animal behavior. Tinbergen identified four overlapping areas of research that lead to different questions about a given pattern of behavior, be it how gazelles run away from lions or how and why dogs play. He suggested that researchers should be interested in 1) the evolution of behavior; 2) adaptation, or how the performance of a specific action allows an individual to fit into his or her environment and ultimately allows the animal to breed; 3) causation, or what causes a particular behavior to occur; and 4) ontogeny, or development, how a behavior arises and unfolds over the course of an individual's life. For example, if I'm interested in how and why dogs play, I'd try to answer the following four questions: 1) What do dogs do when they play and why has play evolved? 2) How does playing allow a dog to adapt to his or her environment, and how does playing influence an individual's reproductive fitness, or output? 3) What causes dogs to play? 4) Finally, how does play develop as individuals get older? I would follow the same line of reasoning if I wanted to know more about grief, pain, or any emotion: I'd ask why they have evolved and what they are good for.

The research methods for answering questions in each of these areas vary, but all begin with careful observation and description of the behavior patterns performed by the animals being studied. The information provided by initial observations allows a researcher to exploit the animal's normal behavioral repertoire to answer questions about the evolution, function, causation, and development of the behavior patterns that are exhibited in various situations. Many people were unsure how to observe and measure behavior because it "just happens and disappears," but Konrad Lorenz, also a curious naturalist, stressed that behavior is something that an animal "has" as well as what he or she "does." It can be thought of in the same way in which we think of an anatomical structure or organ on which natural selection can act. With careful study we can describe an action just as we would a heart or a stomach; we can measure the action and learn why animals perform certain behavior patterns in different situations.

For example, we can ask: What do dogs do when they want to play? How do they insure that play's the name of the game and that dogs around them understand that they are playing? And what do they feel when they play? A play-soliciting action I've studied for years is called the "play bow" or simply the "bow." With careful study we've been able to measure the duration of the bow and how rigid and stereotyped it is. When an animal bows, he or she crouches on the forepaws, elevates the hind end, and may wag the tail. Once you've seen a bow, it's likely you'll recognize it again. Dogs sure do, and they know it means playtime! The bow is often used immediately before and immediately after an action that can be misinterpreted and disrupt ongoing social play (I talk more about play behavior in chapter 4). By filming the bow and watching video frames over and over, we can measure the bow, just like we can measure heart rate or the length of an arm, to find out how many seconds bows last and what they look like. This information is very important for understanding why the bow evolved as a clear and unambiguous signal that's used to tell other animals "I want to play with you."

Tinbergen, Lorenz, and von Frisch used these methods to study phenomena such as imprinting in geese, homing in wasps, hunting by foxes, and dancing in bees. Not only that, they had fun doing so. Lorenz went so far as to don a fox coat and hop along the ground to see how geese would respond to him! Lorenz clearly loved his animal friends, and his groundbreaking work showed that by carefully studying the behavior patterns performed by different organisms (called "comparative research"), we can learn about their evolution and how their performance helped individuals survive. The same detailed analyses and evolutionary arguments can be used for the study of animal emotions.

THE IMPORTANCE OF ANALOGY

However, there is a significant difference between studying hearts and studying "heart." And that is, the heart is a physical object, while emotions and thoughts are "invisible." All we can "see" of an emotion are the signs of it, or how it manifests itself in an animal's behavior or actions and how it affects an animal's neurological chemistry. But rage, love, joy, and grief are not in themselves things that you can hold in your hand.

So ethologists often make their arguments using analogies. They compare humans and other animals and look for similarities (and differences) in any number of features, including brain structure, hormones, physiology, anatomy, and genetics, as well as behavior, facial expressions, vocalizations, and so on. They look at parallels across different species and among different animals of the same species. We are arguing by analogy when we claim that "humans have emotions that can be tied to certain brain structures, and because animals also have the same or similar brain structures, they're experiencing similar emotional states." Indeed, the brains of many species show similar neural organization in some areas involved with emotions. These arguments are thus reasonable because of evolutionary continuity among diverse animal species, including humans.

Joyce Poole, who has studied African elephants for many years, firmly believes that elephants experience pain and suffering, depression, and grief. Poole asks if animals are mere automatons without real emotions, then where did human emotions come from? Certainly there have to be evolutionary precursors to human emotions in other animals unless we believe that human emotions came onto the scene in the absence of any animal ancestors who had emotional lives.

Here is an example of this analogous evolutionary sleuthing in action. Scientist Michel Cabanac has discovered that reptiles, such as iguanas, maximize sensory pleasure. He found that iguanas prefer to stay warm rather than venture out into the cold to get food, whereas amphibians, such as frogs, don't show such behavior. Neither do fish. Iguanas experience what is called "emotional fever" (a rise in body temperature) and tachycardia (increased heart rate), physiological responses that are associated with pleasure in other vertebrates, including humans. Cabanac postulates that the first mental event to emerge into consciousness was the ability of an individual to experience the sensations of pleasure or displeasure. Cabanac's research suggests that reptiles experience basic emotional states, and that the ability to have an emotional life emerged between the time of amphibians and early reptiles.

FIELDWORK:
Getting Down and Dirty

As a rule, ethologists prefer fieldwork to studying animals in a lab. The reason for this is simple: there's simply no substitute for watching animals closely in their natural environment and collecting information on the nitty-gritty details of how they spend their time. If I begin my research, as I often do, with a deceptively simple question like, "What is it like to be a dog in such-and-such situation?" then I must try to understand how dogs get through their days and nights from their dog-centric view of the world. On many occasions I've walked around on all fours, done play bows, howled, barked, bitten their scruffs, and rolled over on my back — though I draw the line at mimicking the all-important hindquarter sniff (I gladly leave that for the dogs). I try to go where the animals live to observe them, and as I study them, I also try to empathize with them. How would I feel if I were in the same situation? Of course, I always remember that *my* view of their world is not necessarily *their* view of their world, but the closer I can get to their view, even by personal analogy, the better I might be able to understand it.

And of course, dogs don't typically live in a lab. In fact, no animal does. Labs can be useful as controlled environments in which to conduct research on how animal minds work, but if you really want to know how animals live, think, and feel from their point of view, then you need to join them in their world. Outside. Also, from an ethologist's perspective, it's important to conduct research in conditions that are as close as possible to the natural environments in which natural selection occurred or is occurring. Finally, the study of captive animals itself raises some difficult questions, ranging from the ethics of performing research on caged animals to questions about the validity of research on stressed individuals who are kept in impoverished conditions. I return to these concerns in chapter 6.

Ultimately, a good ethologist must develop an awareness of all the senses that animals use, and in what combinations in which situations. It is highly unlikely that individuals of any other species sense the world in the same way we do, and it is unlikely that even members of the same species sense the world identically, so it's important to remain alert to the possibility of individual variation. Humans are primarily a visual species, but when considering other animals we need to factor in sounds, odors, and tastes along with visual stimuli. Also, cognitive ethologists emphasize broad comparisons among different species and don't focus on a few select representatives of limited groups of animals, such as rats, mice, or pigeons. Their general commitment to fieldwork rather than the laboratory and their interests in a broad array of animals differentiate cognitive ethologists from psychologists, who are also interested in animal behavior.

PEE, POOP, HAIR, AND GAS:

A Day in the Life of an Ethologist

Fieldwork is about as varied as ethologists themselves. Sometimes it entails sitting back and watching, and sometimes it involves indirect or direct interactions with the animals. When my students and I studied coyotes living in Grand Teton National Park, we sat on Blacktail Butte near Moose, Wyoming, for hours on end using high-powered spotting scopes and binoculars to observe known individuals. But just as often we tracked coyotes on foot, snowshoes, or skis in the cold and dismal dead of winter until we, but not they, were exhausted. When I studied Adélie penguins at Cape Crozier in Antarctica, we ran alongside them as they left their nests and went in and out of the water, and we also sat and froze as they took care of their young and stole rocks from one another in order to build nests. Fieldwork is always interesting, often exhausting, and sometimes not for the squeamish or faint of heart. To end this chapter, I offer two stories of fieldwork involving "yellow snow" and animal dung.

Back at my home in Boulder, I learned about self-awareness in dogs by using an unusual research technique: collecting "yellow snow." Hair, urine, and feces contain a lot of information about who individuals are, who they're related to, what they've eaten, their hormonal and reproductive status, and their emotional state, especially whether or not they're stressed. Scientists can figure these things out using chemical analyses, but animals just use their noses. Indeed, many other animals live in very different sensory worlds from humans. They hear things we can't and smell things we're glad we can't. They inhale deeply and exhale and snort vigorously, sorting a symphony of odors through keenly evolved noses that provide them with important information and great pleasure.

A few years ago I did a study to see what my dog Jethro might know about himself, specifically: Could he tell his urine from that of other dogs? I decided to move Jethro's and other dogs' "yellow snow" from one place to another over the course of five winters. I'd scoop it up in my gloves and set it down in different places so that Jethro would discover it as he cruised on the Boulder bike path where we walked and talked every day. I made sure that he didn't see me do this so he wouldn't know that I was responsible for producing the symphony of odors he was encountering.

I discovered that Jethro showed much more interest in the urine of other dogs than his own. I measured Jethro's interest by the amount of time he spent sniffing the yellow snow and whether or not he sniffed and then peed or "marked" over it. He sniffed and marked over others' urine more, and more so over the urine of other males than the urine of females, even when the samples were moved. Jethro clearly knew what was his and what was others' urine. Most dog owners already know that dogs discriminate their own urine from others', but it turns out that this hadn't before been shown experimentally outside of the laboratory. A simple noninvasive technique confirmed what we knew to be true.

Collecting yellow snow in Colorado is one thing, but what I faced in July 2005, in Kenya, was another. I had the distinct pleasure of collecting elephant dung with George Wittemyer, from the University of California–Berkeley, who was conducting research with Iain Douglas-Hamilton at the Samburu National Reserve in northern Kenya. Perhaps only an adventurous ethologist would respond to the offer, "Hey, you want to help me collect elephant dung?" with an excited yes. I jumped at the opportunity to accompany George, figuring at the very least it would make for great cocktail party conversation when we returned to the States.

We weren't disappointed. A few days before we went dung collecting, as I sat in a truck, a six-year-old female elephant ran toward me, stopped just short of the door, whacked the front of the truck with her trunk, and casually walked away. Then a few hours later, Hewa, a large female elephant who's a member of the group called the Wints, sauntered up to the research vehicle, looked at me as if to say, "Who do you think you are?" and passed wind about two feet from my face. After Hewa's warm welcome, I turned to George and asked, "What's happening?"

"Oh, they're just showing you who's boss in a nice way," he told us. George said that he once had an elephant whack his vehicle with a stick and then flip the stick in the air and walk away. Elephants can flip a truck over on its side if they wish, and this once happened to George and another researcher after a bull male lost a fight. All these stories played through my mind as we sat in the truck a few days later, surrounded by a towering herd of elephants, and waited for them to go to the bathroom.

Now, elephants don't just go on *our* demand, so we sat and sat and sat, and as we waited, George explained these majestic creatures to us: their names, social and genetic relationships, and behaviors. It was fascinating, and awe-inspiring, and best of all, we were conducting research in a noninvasive way that didn't affect the animals' normal behavior. George could have gotten much of the same information by darting and anesthetizing one of the elephants, then drawing and analyzing his or her blood, but how much better for the elephants (and us) to take advantage of their "natural business." Finally, one male decided it was time to go. And did he go! When he was done, George bravely ran in, disappeared among the towering elephants (who didn't seem to notice him at all), scooped the huge pile of feces into a plastic bag, ran back to the truck, and threw the bag in the rear. He was smiling all the way. I was too, but I also couldn't wait to get rid of the bag back at the camp. This sample of dung and others like it were then sent off for genetic analyses, which help George and his colleagues further understand the elephants at Samburu.

Elephants are the poster species for animal emotions, since they display so many so deeply. But emotions have evolved in many other species as well. Let's now go explore the passionate lives of animals.

CHAPTER 3

Beastly Passions: What Animals Feel

Much of chimpanzees' nonverbal communication is similar to ours. When greeting after an absence, they may kiss, embrace, or pat each other on the back. In aggressive incidents, they may swagger, scowl, scream, punch, slap, or kick. There are strong, affectionate bonds between individuals, particularly mothers and offspring, and maternal siblings, that may persist throughout life.... They show emotions clearly similar to those we label happy, sad, angry, and depressed.

— JANE GOODALL AND RAY GREEK

At a talk I was giving, someone once asked me if I knew of a good field guide to animal emotions, and I told them to ask their mail carrier or delivery person. My UPS deliveryman, Dave, can read dogs better than most people I know, and he will tell you with no hesitation that dogs experience a host of deep feelings, which they express to him daily.

Animals feel a wide range of emotions, including each of Darwin's six universal emotions: anger, happiness, sadness, disgust, fear, and surprise. If we can observe some of these emotions better than others, this probably has more to do with the subtlety of certain feelings than with the expressiveness of animals. For when animals are happy, they feel true

Happiness with a capital *H*, and when sad, they experience Grief with a capital *G*. Indeed, when we pay attention, animals display a mindful presence, unfiltered emotions, and a zest for life.

In this chapter, I look at seven emotions in animals, mainly mammals for whom the database is the most substantive; some emotions are obvious and some are subtle. We witness animals loudly sharing their joy, anger, grief, and love. We try to discern whether animals can feel embarrassment and awe. And though it's rarely the focus of scientific research, we observe animals making jokes, or displaying a sense of humor. As my deliveryman will attest, this list of emotions is by no means exhaustive. In fact, there's every reason to believe that many animals feel just as many emotions as humans do.

That said, it's important to remember that there are differences among species in how they express their emotions (as well as perhaps in what they feel), and that there are also differences among individuals of the same species. Not all dogs or chimpanzees experience and express joy, grief, or jealousy in the same way. Research by Sam Gosling and his colleagues has shown that, as with humans, each individual has his or her own "personality." Animals can be bold, shy, playful, aggressive, sociable, curious, emotionally stable, or agreeable; they can be extroverted, introverted, dominant, or submissive. Individual and species differences make the study of animal emotions more difficult and challenging, but they also make it more exciting. As the saying goes, it takes all kinds of people to make the world go round, and the same is true about the different "personalities" within the social world of animals.

SEEING FEELINGS:

A Short Field Guide to Observing Emotions

In fact, it is sometimes easier to see and understand emotions in animals than in humans because animals do not filter their emotions. What they feel is clearly written on their faces, made public by tails, ears, and odors, and displayed by their actions. Animal emotions are raw and out there for all to see, hear, smell, and feel. Anyone can tell. For some, like my UPS man, it's even an occupational necessity.

The one main caveat is that identifying emotions is different from understanding the social behavior of animals. When dogs play, it's easy to see their joy, but it takes training, experience, and research to correctly interpret the complex interactions and behaviors involved in the expression of that joy, such as the "play bow" I describe in chapter 2. The cover of this book shows another kind of social gesture: Motomo, a mid-ranking black wolf, is licking the face of Kamots — the highest ranking, or alpha, male of the pack. This gesture is a display of submission, and such behavior is used to reinforce social bonds and helps maintain the unity of the pack. We can readily see affection (as opposed to aggression) in the gesture, but without knowing the relationship of these particular wolves, or the dynamics of their pack, it would be difficult to know whether that lick was friendly, romantic, or motherly; whether it was meant to groom, mollify, or comfort.

Indeed, in social species like wolves, where a pack needs to run like a well-oiled engine, we usually see more nuanced emotions — individuals need to know not only what others are doing or planning to do, but also what they're feeling. If we compare highly social wolves to less social coyotes and dogs, we find that wolves have more varied facial expressions, and that they use these expressions to communicate their emotional states to others. Wolf tails are also more expressive, and wolves use more tail positions than do dogs or coyotes to express their emotions.

Nevertheless, it is surprisingly easy to recognize basic or primary emotions in animals. All we have to do is look, listen, and smell. Their faces, their eyes, and the ways in which they carry themselves can be used to make strong inferences about what they are feeling. Changes in muscle tone, posture, gait, facial expression, eye size and gaze, vocalizations, and odors (pheromones), singly and together, all indicate emotional responses to certain situations. A person doesn't even need to be consciously aware of these aspects; from simply watching an animal, people can often intuitively sense the correct emotion.

Extensive research by Françoise Wemelsfelder and her colleagues has verified this; they've conducted a variety of studies that show that even regular folks (as opposed to trained scientists) can do a consistently accurate job of identifying animal emotions. We tend to think that our personal impressions are too subjective, and therefore must not be right, but when it comes to emotions, Wemelsfelder and her associates have found that we are actually very often correct.

Wemelsfelder uses what she calls "Free-Choice-Profiling." To quote Professor Wemelsfelder:

> The question is whether people agree in the judgments they make, and whether they can use these judgments as a scientific assessment tool. So we gathered various groups of untrained observers, and asked them to watch a number of individual animals interact with a human person for some time. The animals we worked with were mostly pigs; pigs are lively, inquisitive, highly social animals that actively interact with their environment when given the chance. The observers were asked to... write down the words that in their view best summed up the pigs' expressions. The freedom to create one's own terms was crucial, because it required observers to integrate what they saw for themselves, rather than be prejudiced and limited by a list of given terms.

Wemelsfelder has been testing her Free-Choice-Profiling for years and has found that it works and could in fact be used as an assessment tool by researchers. Wemelsfelder says: "Whether observers were students, scientists, pig farmers, veterinarians or animal rights activists, we persistently found high levels of agreement (both within and between these groups) in how they judged the pigs. With their personal terminologies, observers created coherent and meaningful semantic frameworks that they could use to characterize the expression of individual pigs in precise and repeatable ways."

Other researchers have come to the same conclusion: whether people are observing wolves, dogs, or cats, they discern emotions nearly as well as trained researchers. This means that either animal emotions are just not that well hidden or humans have a natural ability to discern emotions in other species. I'm willing to bet it's a little of both. Indeed, try it yourself the next time you go to the park. What do you think those dogs are feeling? Here are a few things to pay attention to.

Love Is in the Air

Another way that animals communicate how they feel is through their scent. Scientists may not be very adept at using their noses, but not so other animals. Scent can be a very powerful communicator, as is made clear in the following vivid description of a male elephant experiencing what is called "musth":

> He is a hot-blooded, 30-year-old male in peak physical condition. He has mucus oozing from his cheeks and green urine streaming down his legs. His penis has a green sheen to it and he gives off a smell that can be picked up half a mile away. He wafts his ears back and forth and makes a low rumble. He looks confident: after all, many females find him irresistible. Sounds familiar? Hopefully not. He is a male elephant in musth — something like a state of rut. Sexually mature bull elephants go through musth for a one to two-month period every year. They don't exactly hide it, excreting a cocktail of chemicals from a bulbous gland on their cheeks that can swell to the size of a basketball, passing more than 300 litres of urine a day (equivalent to 24 buckets), and — not surprisingly — smelling like a herd of goats. What's more, during this dramatic advertisement of his sexuality the male appears to undergo something of a personality change; indeed, the word musth is derived from a Persian word meaning drunk. They become very aggressive and obsessed with sex, probably as a result of their high testosterone levels, which can increase by up to 60 times.

A male elephant in musth isn't an animal with whom you'd want to cross paths. What's interesting here is not only are there rapid and obvious personality changes during musth, but also that a male in musth can communicate his intentions clearly and openly to females in whom he's interested, as well as put other males on alert. "Musth is the elephant version of expensive aftershave and a flash car. It is thought to inform males and females alike of an elephant's age, status and reproductive health, and also increases a male's chances of reproductive success."

The chemical that does it all is called frontalin, which is secreted by sweat glands in the elephant's cheeks and also shows up in the animal's breath and urine. A male proclaims his intentions and prowess, females assess his reproductive fitness, and other males judge how strong he is before picking a fight. The precision of this signaling seems to be unique among mammals, but it's likely that nonmammals also use odors to show their intentions.

About Face

Faces are also extremely important in assessing animal feelings. Charles Darwin and later researchers have stressed the importance of facial expressions in our understanding of others' emotions. Recently, it was decided that Leonardo da Vinci's *Mona Lisa* was actually happy. A computer program using emotion recognition software at the University of Amsterdam used the curvature of the lips and the crinkles around her eyes to make this determination. She may even have been pregnant or had just given birth. While I can't say I agree, faces are nonetheless important for inferring what others are feeling and for predicting what they're likely to do in the future. Researchers have found that mammals share a great number of facial expressions, which makes it possible to infer what a monkey is feeling in the same way we can we see what an actress in a silent movie is expressing. We clearly can read the facial expressions of dogs and their wild relatives — submissive grimaces, toothy growls, open-mouth play pants — in a wide variety of social situations.

Some animals — like reptiles, fish, and birds — lack expressive faces. This can make it harder for us to interpret their feelings, but this doesn't mean that they're not feeling anything. In fact compelling data stemming from behavioral and neurobiological studies show that fish are conscious, intelligent, and sentient beings who express preferences. They're not merely streams of dietary proteins. And as we see below, birds don't need lips or eyebrows to be expressive with their emotions.

Look into My Eyes

> *The elephants came at all times of the year.... Sometimes they turned their giant rumps to our thatched roof and scratched their thick hides on the rough grass, closing their eyes in what appeared to be the most blissful glee.* — DELIA OWENS, *SECRETS OF THE SAVANNA*

> *But most disturbing of all, in Blue's large brown eyes was a new look, more painful than the look of despair: the look of disgust with human beings, with life; the look of hatred.*
>
> — ALICE WALKER, "AM I BLUE?"

Of course, when we speak of faces, many times what we are really talking about are the eyes. Eyes are magnificently complex organs that provide a window into an individual's emotional world. As in humans, in many species eyes reflect feelings, whether wide open in glee or sunken in despair. Eyes are mysterious, evocative, and immediate communicators.

Doug Smith, who leads the Yellowstone wolf reintroduction project, recently wrote about looking into the eyes of a wolf named Five: "The last time I looked into Five's eyes... she was walking away from an elk her pack had killed.... As we flew overhead, she looked up at us, as she always did. But the look she gave me had changed. To gaze into the eyes of a wild wolf is one of the holiest of grails for lovers of nature; some say what you see is untamed, unspoiled wildness.... That day in January, something had gone out of Five's eyes; she looked worried. Always before her gaze had been defiant."

Reading emotions in eyes is not as clear-cut as reading gestures like the play bow. Personal interpretation or intuition plays a role, and yet there is no more direct animal-to-animal communication than staring deeply into another's eyes. Even when we can't measure their meaning, it is the eyes that most evocatively convey sentience. Charles Siebert, in a 2006 *New York Times Magazine* essay, wrote about the "unsettling black eyes" of Achilles, a giant Pacific octopus. "It was those eyes more than anything that I had asked [Roland] Anderson for special permission to come back and stare into on my own. Just me and Achilles."

An animal's gaze can be unflinching, and when an animal is in need, his or her eyes sometimes tell us all we need to know. For instance, eyes played a central role in the well-known story of Rick Swope and JoJo. While standing outside the chimpanzee enclosure at the Detroit Zoo, Rick watched as JoJo, an older 130-pound adult male chimpanzee, ran into the enclosure's moat to escape from an aggressive young male. As JoJo began to drown, Rick jumped in to save him. Three other adult male chimpanzees then began to threaten Rick, and he had to get out, but he returned moments later and succeeded in rescuing JoJo. Rick did this despite repeated warnings that his life was in danger, and when asked why, he answered: "I looked into his eyes. It was like looking into the eyes of a man. And the message was: Won't *anybody* help me?" Recently, three men near my hometown of Boulder tried to save a young mountain lion who'd been hit by a car. They told reporters that the lions' eyes begged them to do so — saying the same thing: "Help me."

A recent study, looking at fear in humans, confirms the importance of eye contact in recognizing emotions. It turns out that the eyes are of paramount importance in knowing that another human is feeling fear, and that people tend to look at the eyes to know when a face is fearful. The study looked at a woman who had damage to a region of her brain (the amygdala) that caused her to fail to recognize fearful facial expressions.

They found the reason she couldn't perceive fear was because she didn't look spontaneously toward the eyes. Therefore, she judged a fearful face as having a neutral expression. As these stories about animals make clear, the eyes are important in perceiving fear in animals as well, and it's quite likely that the eyes are important in perceiving other emotions.

In fact, the eyes of a cat were instrumental in my development as a scientist. A doctoral research project I was once involved in required us to kill the cats we were studying. However, when I went to get "Speedo," a very intelligent cat that I'd secretly named — secretly, because we weren't supposed to name "subjects" — for the final exit from his cage, his fearlessness disappeared as if he knew that this was his last journey. As I picked him up, he looked at me and asked, "Why me?" Tears came to my eyes. He wouldn't break his piercing stare. Though I followed through with what I was supposed to do and killed him, it broke my heart to do so. To this day I remember his unwavering eyes — they told the whole story of the interminable pain and indignity he had endured. Others in the program tried to reassure me that it was all worth it, but I never recovered from that experience.

So I left the program and entered another one in which naming was not only permitted but actively encouraged, and I resolved not to conduct research that involved intentionally inflicting pain or causing the death of another being.

A Wink and a Nuzzle: Expressions of Gratitude

Identifying emotions with scientific rigor can be tricky, and to do so, researchers usually consider the total sum of actions, behaviors, and expressions they're seeing, as well as the larger context of the situation. Even then, gut feelings can come into play. For instance, can a whale say thanks? Listen to this story and see what you think.

In December 2005 a fifty-foot fifty-ton female humpback whale got tangled up in crab lines, the weight of which was making it difficult for her to keep her blow hole above the water. A courageous team of divers freed her, and after being freed the whale nuzzled each of her saviors in turn and flapped around in what one whale expert said was "a rare and remarkable encounter." James Moskito, one of the rescuers, immediately recognized that the whale was in trouble: "My heart sank when I saw all the lines wrapped around it." As for what happened afterward, he recalled, "It felt to me like it was thanking us, knowing it was free and that we had helped it." He said the whale "stopped about a foot away from me, pushed me around a little bit and had some fun." And during the rescue, he said, "When I was cutting the line going through the mouth, its eye was there winking at me, watching me.... It was an epic moment of my life."

One of the other rescuers, Mike Menigoz, was also deeply touched by the encounter: "You hate to anthropomorphize too much, but the whale was doing little dives and the guys were rubbing shoulders with it.... I don't know for sure what it was thinking, but it's something I will always remember. It was just too cool."

In this life-changing encounter, the divers expressed feeling deep sympathy and empathy for the female whale's suffering, and they describe actions by the whale that, in this context, could very well be reactions to such kindness: leviathan expressions of gratitude. We also see that it's very natural to attribute "human" feelings to animals. Indeed, the only language the divers had to describe the whale's actions was from the field of human emotion. And yet, even if our human terms are imperfect descriptions of the whale's actual emotions, does that mean the whale wasn't feeling anything? Is there another credible explanation?

In fact, another explanation appeared in print not long after this encounter. In a follow-up story in *Reader's Digest*, Frances Gulland, a veterinarian at the Marine Mammal Center in Sausalito, California, is quoted as saying that the whale probably swam in circles because her body had been kinked for so long. The divers just happened to be there while she was exercising.

Since not a single rescuer felt that the whale was "exercising," we must decide for ourselves whether the rescuers were simply projecting feelings of gratitude on an unfeeling animal, or whether they intuitively understood the whale's unfamiliar emotional gestures. I address this question of anthropomorphizing — what it is and whether it's bad — in much more detail in chapter 5. However, what we're learning is that hard science is confirming what our intuitions so often tell us: animals express emotions in ways we are naturally able to understand.

JOY WITH A CAPITAL J

Much research has been done on the negative emotions — boredom, pain, fear, anger — but now more attention is being given to the positive emotions (such as joy and pleasure), which, like some of the negative emotions, are rooted in areas of the ancient limbic system shared among many different mammals. Paul Ekman, a leader in the study of human emotion and facial expression, agrees with Darwin that "the pursuit of enjoyment is a primary emotion in our lives." If this is true for us, it should also be true for other animals.

To observe animals for any length of time is to see that animals clearly enjoy themselves. Animals experience immense joy in a wide range of situations: when they play, greet friends, groom one another, are freed from confinement, sing, and perhaps even when watching others having fun. Joy is so contagious, it's essentially an epidemic. One researcher tells of watching a female chimpanzee give birth, after which her closest friend screamed and embraced two other chimps. The friend then tended the mother and her offspring for several weeks.

Joy and happiness are clearly signaled by behavior — animals are relaxed and walk loosely, as if their arms and legs are attached to their bodies by rubber bands. They also speak in their own tongues — purring, barking, or squealing in contentment. Dolphins chuckle when they are happy. Greeting ceremonies in African wild dogs involve cacophonies of squealing, propeller-like tail wagging, and bounding gaits.

When coyotes or wolves reunite, they gallop toward one another whining and smiling, their tails wagging wildly. Upon meeting, they lick one another's muzzles, roll over, and flail their legs. When elephants reunite, there is a raucous celebration. They flap their ears, spin about, and emit a "greeting rumble." If this behavior does not signal unashamed jubilation, then what is it — just more exercising?

According to Rosamund Young in her book *The Secret Life of Cows*, even hens love to play, and they're smart, moody, emotional, and form close friendships. Although it's easy to see that chickens suffer from pain and discomfort caused by various methods of industrial farming — foot lesions, bone breakage, beak trimming, feather pecking, cannibalism, joint problems — it's more difficult to know if they're happy. But it's entirely reasonable to posit that they, like other animals, enjoy playing. Young notes that cows also play games with one another and form strong life-long friendships. She says they also sulk, hold grudges, and act vain.

As the ethologist, animal advocate, and author Jonathan Balcombe points out, evolution favors sensory rewards because they drive beings to stay alive and reproduce. We prefer what gives us pleasure, so evolution has made what we need to do pleasurable. To quote Balcombe:

> For too long scientists have denied the existence of positive sensory experiences in other species because we cannot know for certain what another being feels. But in the absence of compelling evidence to the contrary, it is more reasonable to assume that other creatures, who share so much in common with us through our shared evolutionary origins, do, in fact, experience pleasure. We cannot feel the hummingbird's response to a trumpet-flower's nectar, the dog's anticipation of chasing a ball, or the turtle's experience of basking in the sun, but we can imagine those feelings based on our own experiences of similar situations. What we can observe in animals, combined with our capacity to empathize from our own experience, leaves little doubt that the animal kingdom is a rich repository of pleasure. And as

we grow to accept and acknowledge the pleasure that attends animals' lives, evidence for it will proliferate, for we are more likely to find something when we are looking for it.

Evidence of joy in animals is already so extensive that it should hardly need further discussion. At a meeting on animal sentience that I attended in 2005, John Webster, a professor of animal husbandry at the University of Bristol, said, "Sentient animals have the capacity to experience pleasure and are motivated to seek it.... You only have to watch how cows and lambs both seek and enjoy pleasure when they lie with their heads raised to the sun on a perfect English summer's day. Just like humans."

Jonathan Balcombe also provides a nice example:

> During a recent trip to Assateague, Virginia, I watched two fish crows (*Corvus ossifragus*) land on an old wooden billboard that protruded incongruously from a cattail marsh. Hoping they would stay awhile, I swiveled my telescope and focused on them. They first engaged in flight play, then over the next 10 minutes, one bird (always the same one) repeatedly sidled up to the other, leaned over, and pointed his/her beak down, exposing the nape. The other bird responded by gently sweeping his/her bill through the feathers as though searching for parasites. There was every indication that they were mates or good buddies, and that their contact was as pleasurable for both giver and receiver, as a massage or caress between two humans.

Joy in animals may be obvious to one's eyes, but it is also confirmed by neurobiological studies, or "hard science," on the effects of play and laughter.

The Chemistry of Play

Social play is an excellent example of a behavior that both feels good and is important for survival. The shared joy experienced during play connects individuals and regulates interactions. Play is easy to discern from other behaviors: Individuals become deeply immersed in the activity and show their delight by their acrobatic movements, gleeful vocalizations, and smiles. They play hard, get exhausted, rest, and go at it again and again.

Studies of the chemistry of play support the idea that play is fun. Neuroscientist Steve Siviy has shown that dopamine (and perhaps serotonin and norepinephrine) is important in the regulation of play, and that large regions of the brain are active during play. Rats show an increase in dopamine activity simply anticipating the opportunity to play.

These findings suggest that there are neurochemical bases for why play is enjoyable, and that the same chemical changes occur in both animals and humans during play. In other words, a boy and his dog wrestling in the yard are not only both playing — they both understand that they're playing, and they're getting the same pleasurable feelings from doing so.

Having a Laugh

Laughter clearly isn't uniquely human. There's also solid scientific information showing that dogs laugh — there's what researcher Patricia Simonet calls "a breathy, pronounced, forced exhalation" heard when dogs are excited and when they play. Simonet discovered that the sounds of dog laughter could also soothe other dogs who hear them even if they're not playing. Rats also chirp with joy, and there's little doubt that future research will show this to be true in many other animals.

Jane Goodall noted that female chimpanzees occasionally will use sticks to tickle their genitals and laugh as they're doing it. Laughing, or vocalizations such as play pants, might be responsible for the reciprocity of social play. Primatologist Takahisha Matsusaka has shown that play panting during social play in wild chimpanzees encourages continuation of tickling or chasing and reduces the risk of play escalating into aggression. And Robert Provine suggests that laughter actually evolved from labored breathing due to physical play, and it likely signals "I like it, do it again."

Neural circuits for laughter can be found in very ancient regions of the brain. As neuroscientist Jaak Panksepp notes, "Research on roughhousing play in mammals, both sapient and otherwise, clearly indicates that the sources of play and laughter in the brain are both instinctual and subcortical." The neurochemical dopamine is also implicated in both human and rat laughter.

Panksepp says, "Tickles are the key.... They open up a previously hidden world." Rats who are tickled bond to the researchers and seek out tickles. Their feelings indeed function as social glue. Rats laugh only when they're feeling good, in the same sense that animals play only when all is well.

"It's like the behavior of young children," says Robert Provine. "A tickle and laughter are the first means of communication between a mother and her baby, so laughter appears by about four months after birth."

In humans, the importance of such an early behavior is apparent, so it shouldn't be a surprise to find that it's equally important among other animals. As it turns out, there's nothing frivolous about the study of animal laughter. But do animals know any good jokes?

STAND-UP COMEDIANS:
Animals with a Sense of Humor

It's one thing to discover the neurochemicals responsible for the feelings of joy and happiness in animals, but how do we distinguish and correctly identify subtler, more deliberate thoughts and emotions? If animals can laugh, does that mean they can tell jokes? Many pet owners will nod affirmatively: they know for themselves that animals have what we call a sense of humor. Farmers know to be wary around their donkeys. My late canine companion, Jethro, used to run all over with his favorite toy, a stuffed rabbit, in his mouth. He'd scoop it up on the run, bound here and there, and then turn to see if anyone was watching. If they were, he'd continue his frantic game. My friends and I would always laugh, which apparently was the reward Jethro was looking for.

Other anecdotal evidence seems to confirm that animals not only know how to have fun, they know how to make fun, tell jokes, and engage in slapstick comedy. The following three stories were told to me by friends.

Jill Robinson — the founder of Animals Asia who rescued Jasper, the moon bear to whom this book is dedicated — shared with me further stories about the moon bears she has rescued. She writes:

> The moon bears will often gang up together against another bear — in fact we have one female group of bears we affectionately call the 'knitting circle' because they remind us so much of elderly ladies who seemingly have nothing better to do but gossip the day away and who will join together to warn away another bear who comes too close to their exclusive circle. Such friendships for a species recognized to be solitary in the wild are extraordinary. Often, one bear will wait until another is distracted and then steal toys or food away — in every sense like a greedy sibling, biding their time until the opportunity arises to steal from a brother or sister. Their sense of fun and mischief finally wins through all but the most severe legacy of pain and stress.

Mim Eichler Rivas wrote a wonderful book about "the world's smartest horse" entitled *Beautiful Jim Key: The Lost History of a Man and Horse Who Changed the World*. She says that the horse, Beautiful Jim Key, had an amazing sense of humor, and that this was attested to "by everyone from skeptical reporters to doting human family members to presidents, senators, mayors, and even the team of Harvard professors who were sent to assess just how smart he was."

Mim wrote the following note to me:

> Perhaps they could explain away some of his apparent intellectual feats — 'reading,' 'writing,' and 'rithmetic' — as the result of rote repetition or some system of guidance provided by

> his human companion, Dr. William Key. For when Jim started to imitate the dogs — fetching sticks and sitting at attention, rolling over, and playing dead — the laughter that the Doc provided was clearly his reward.
>
> Yet what caught the Doc off-guard was when Jim created his own bits — like the time when a man in a crowd offered to buy Jim for five hundred dollars, and Dr. Key pretended to consider it, causing a healthy, strapping Jim Key to suddenly go lame and attempt to play dead. When Dr. Key said he'd never sell Jim, the Equine Thespian sprang right back up again. It was often his humor and his charm that changed the mind of hard-boiled reporters. Dr. Key often arranged for reporters to visit with Jim alone and ask him to spell words with his spelling board or make change from his cash register, and so on. The reporters were reminded that Jim was a celebrity and liked to be brought a special treat, perhaps an apple or pear tucked in a pocket. One reporter for the Post Standard forgot to bring anything, and after Dr. Key let the reporter and Jim have some time alone, he returned and asked Jim, 'Well, how did it go?' Jim began to spell, drawing letters one by one and lining them up on his spelling stand, until he had spelled the word 'F-R-U-I-T-L-E-S-S.' That reporter claimed that he was instantly a true believer.

Renowned filmmaker and writer Michael Tobias told me about his family's large scarlet macaw, who Michael and his wife, Jane, have taken care of for decades. Actually, Michael says they serve this magnificent and rare emperor of an avian on their proverbial hands and knees, and he claims that the bird — whose name Michael would not deign to translate into mere English — apparently wields more verb tenses than most highly literate *Homo sapiens* and is endowed with a macaw vocabulary that defies casual analysis. He also, it seems, is endowed with an infectious sense of humor and sport.

The macaw giggles, chuckles, and roars with laughter; he teases all who come near, squeals with delight when running around the house, bounds up and down on trees outside, and even plays "magic carpet" — wherein his human slaves race down hallways dragging large towels with the macaw riding aboard. Michael has observed laughter in numerous parrot species — as well as in a host of other birds — but he believes parrots may be among the greatest wits on the planet. Not only do they laugh, but they display perfect timing. If the macaw lobs a small Frisbee at Michael with his enormous beak and hits Michael in the face, or if Michael misses it, the macaw nearly falls over in hysterics. With a specific knowledge of where people are ticklish, the macaw then charges Michael's underarm so as to goose him until Michael himself is in tears laughing.

And what does Michael make of all this? He writes,

> If a bird, whose kind are headed to extinction given current rates of human trespass and insanity; a bird that will outlive most individual humans; one whose intelligence far surpasses most ungainly, carnivorous, indifferent *Homo sapiens*; can nonetheless find humor in the madness of the world, share joy with the few people it trusts, then we must take heed before the awesome innocence that the rest of creation is endeavoring to offer up by way of an example. If we fail to appreciate, even worship the laughter of macaws, or to engage in the dialogue that the animal kingdom is extending to us; or, finally, to be quiet, humble, and serene before the sheer miracle of life, then we will indeed go down in biological history as the worst, meanest, shortest-lived failure in the history of evolution. We would be wise indeed to take the lesson of a forgiving macaw to heart, and none too soon.

CHIMPANZEES AND WATERFALLS:
Awe and Wonder

If animals can display such humorous delight in other beings, is it also possible that they might, at times, marvel at their surroundings and feel a sense of awe at the world? Do they experience the joy of simply being alive? And if so, how would that express itself? Wild animals spend upward of 90 percent of their time resting: What are they thinking and feeling as they gaze about? It would be nice to know. Again, science may never be able to measure such emotions with any precision, but anecdotal evidence and careful observation indicate feelings akin to wonder may exist.

Sometimes animals "just go nuts," as one of my students once commented. Indeed, when we were at Lake Nakuru in Kenya, in July 2005, we watched a young black rhinoceros "go nuts" — he ran all over the place like he was having a fit, while his mother watched him with a careful eye all the time. What was causing him to act with such abandon? We don't know. There was no cause we could see other than that it felt good. There were no other potential playmates around, or for that matter no other rhinos except for his mother.

Then there are chimpanzee waterfall dances, which are a delight to witness. Sometimes a chimpanzee, usually an adult male, will dance at a waterfall with total abandon. Why? The actions are deliberate but obscure. Could it be they are a joyous response to being alive, or even an expression of the chimp's awe of nature? Where, after all, might human spiritual impulses originate? Jane Goodall wonders whether these dances are indicative of religious behavior, precursors of religious ritual. She describes a chimpanzee approaching one of these falls with slightly bristled hair, a sign of heightened arousal: "As he gets closer, and the roar of the falling water gets louder, his pace quickens, his hair becomes fully erect, and upon reaching the stream he may perform a magnificent display close to the foot of the falls. Standing upright, he sways rhythmically from foot to foot, stamping in the shallow, rushing water, picking up and hurling great rocks. Sometimes he climbs up the slender vines that hang down from the trees high above and swings out into the spray of the falling water. This 'waterfall dance' may last ten or fifteen minutes." Chimpanzees also dance at the onset of heavy rains and during violent gusts of wind. Goodall asks, "Is it not possible that these performances are stimulated by feelings akin to wonder and awe? After a waterfall display the performer may sit on a rock, his eyes following the falling water. What is it, this water?"

Goodall wonders, "If the chimpanzee could share his feelings and questions with others, might these wild elemental displays become ritualized into some form of animistic religion? Would they worship the falls, the deluge from the sky, the thunder and lightning — the gods of the elements? So all-powerful; so incomprehensible."

Goodall admits that she'd love to get into their minds even for a few moments. It would be worth years of research to discover what animals see and feel when they look at the stars. In June 2006, Jane and I visited the Mona Foundation's chimpanzee sanctuary near Girona, Spain. We were told that Marco, one of the rescued chimpanzees, does a dance during thunderstorms in which he looks like he's in a trance. Perhaps numerous animals engage in these rituals but we haven't been lucky enough to see them.

Like Jane, I too would love to get into the mind and heart of a dog or a wolf, even if I couldn't tell anyone about it afterward — what an amazing experience it would be.

GRIEF AND SADNESS

Tragedy struck in 1997. Fourteen's mate, Thirteen, was much older than she... In March, his collar emitted the accelerated series of beeps that signals a dead wolf. After that, Fourteen took off. She traveled west through inhospitable terrain that she had never ventured into before.... Eventually Fourteen made her way back to her family.... No one, including myself, wanted to suggest that she had traveled alone so far because she was mourning the loss of her mate. But she never bred again even though she consorted with other mature males.

— DOUG SMITH, "MEET FIVE, NINE, AND FOURTEEN, YELLOWSTONE'S HEROINE WOLVES"

There is no question that animals grieve, and as the stories in this section show, the universal signs of grief are seen most keenly when animals respond to the death of a mate, family member, or friend. Like humans, animals can suffer monumentally over a separation or loss. Grieving animals may withdraw from their group and seek seclusion, resistant to all attempts by others to draw them out. They may sit in one place, motionless, staring vacantly into space. They stop eating and lose interest in sex. Sometimes they become obsessed with the dead individual. They may try to revive him or her, and failing that, remain with the carcass for days on end. Janet Baker-Carr writes in *An Extravagance of Donkeys* that these wonderful beasts of burden show concern when a group member becomes ill. The author tells about the death of a female, and how the other donkeys stood on her grave and brayed a sad requiem long into the night.

Humans and animals share neural pathways when it comes to suffering. Some scientists even say that the demeanor of elephants suffering from the loss of friends and the disruption of social bonds resembles post-traumatic stress disorder (PTSD). Recently, scientists have identified a part of the brain associated with PTSD, called the ventromedial prefrontal cortex; activity in this part of the brain varies among people, making some more prone to anxiety, fear, and stress than others. In animals this structure seems to be important with helping the brain to forget.

Grief itself is something of a mystery, for there doesn't seem to be any obvious adaptive value to it in an evolutionary sense. It does not seem to increase an individual's reproductive success. Some theorize that perhaps mourning strengthens social bonds among survivors who band together to pay their last respects. This may enhance group cohesion at a time when it's likely to be weakened. Whatever its value is, grief is the price of commitment, that wellspring of both happiness and sorrow.

A Fox Funeral

One evening when I was driving up my road, I saw a large tan animal walking toward my car. I thought it was my neighbor Robb's German shepherd, Lolo, so I stopped and opened the car door to say hello. As I came face to face with a big male mountain lion, only then did I hear Lolo barking behind me. The lion stared at me, seemed to shrug his shoulders, and walked off, as if to say, "Silly human." I was so scared, I slammed the door shut, went home, and ran straight to my house.

The next morning Robb told me that Lolo had found the carcass of a red fox, and I went to look at it. The fox, a formerly very healthy male, had obviously been killed by the lion, and his body was partially covered with branches, dirt, and some of the fox's own fur.

Two mornings later, I waited until it was fully light and headed out to hike with Jethro. (No more surprises for me!) I looked down the road and saw a small female red fox trying to cover the carcass. I was fascinated, for she was deliberately orienting her body so that when she kicked debris with her hind legs, it would cover her friend, perhaps her mate. A family of foxes has lived near my house for almost a decade, and it's very likely she was related to, or at least a close friend of, the dead fox. She'd kick dirt, stop, look at the carcass, and intentionally kick again. I observed this "ritual" for about a minute. Afterward, the female continued to slink around the carcass with her tail down. A few hours later, I returned to the carcass and found it totally buried.

Had I just seen a fox funeral? It looked to me as if the female fox was trying to bury the dead fox. Her actions and her manner certainly reflected sadness and grief. I was lucky to see what I did. Much happens in the complex lives of animals that we can't see — and will never be able to re-create in a lab — and when we're fortunate to observe animals at work, it is a splendid event that can reveal much about their innermost feelings.

Gorilla Wakes and Baboon Friendships

Gorillas are known to hold wakes for dead friends, something that some zoos have formalized in a ceremony when one of their gorillas passes away. Donna Fernandes, director of the Buffalo Zoo, tells the story of being at Boston's Franklin Park Zoo ten years ago during the wake for a female gorilla, Babs, who had died of cancer. She describes seeing the gorilla's longtime mate say good-bye: "He was howling and banging his chest, . . . and he picked up a piece of her favorite food — celery — and put it in her hand and tried to get her to wake up. I was weeping, it was so emotional." Later, the scene at Babs's December funeral was similarly moving. As reported by the local news, gorilla family members "one by one . . . filed into" the room where "Babs's body lay," approaching their "beloved leader" and "gently sniffing the body."

Primates, being near relatives to humans, often exhibit behavior remarkably close to us. In addition to gorillas holding wakes, baboons are known to seek the comfort of friends after deaths in their family. Researchers from the University of Pennsylvania report that baboons rely on friendships to help them cope with stressful situations. In their study, when a lion killed a baboon named Sierra, her mother, Sylvia, looked to friends for support. Says researcher Anne Engh, "With Sierra gone, Sylvia experienced what could only really be described as depression, corresponding with an increase in her glucocorticoid levels."

When baboons experience stress they show an increase in hormones called glucocorticoids, just as humans do. These hormones are produced by the adrenal gland. Baboons can lower their glucocorticoid levels through friendly social contact, by expanding their social network after the loss of specific close companions. "Without Sierra, Sylvia really had nobody else," Engh says. "So great was her need for social bonding that Sylvia began grooming with a female of a much lower status, behavior that would otherwise be beneath her."

Engh concludes somewhat cautiously: "Our findings do not necessarily suggest that baboons experience grief like humans do, but they do offer evidence of the importance of social bonds amongst baboons. Like humans, baboons seem to rely on friendly relationships to help them cope with stressful situations."

Dying of a Broken Heart

Many years ago, veterinarian Marty Becker gave his father a miniature schnauzer, Pepsi, as a gift. Marty told me that he had helped to deliver Pepsi, who was the runt of his litter, and the dog became his father's best friend. For years they shared the same food, the same chair, and the same bed. Then, when he was eighty years old, Marty's father committed suicide. Soon after family, friends, and the police left his house, Pepsi ran downstairs to the spot in the basement where Marty's father had died and stood as rigid as a statue. When Marty picked Pepsi up, the dog went from rigid to limp in his arms and emitted a painful moan. Marty put him in his father's bed and Pepsi immediately fell asleep. Marty later found out from his mother that Pepsi hadn't been in the basement for ten years because he was afraid of steps. Had Pepsi overcome his fear in order to say good-bye to his lifelong friend? Pepsi never recovered from his companion's death. Remaining weak and withdrawn, he slowly died. When Marty buried Pepsi, he was convinced that Pepsi had indeed died of a broken heart: he'd lost the will to live once the human to whom he was so closely bonded and devoted was no longer around.

An Elephant Burial

Elephants are well known for the deep concern and curiosity they show for dead individuals. It's rare to witness elephants coping with their dead, so it's difficult to collect detailed data, but numerous observations show time and again that elephants are concerned with suffering and death and openly show compassion when encountering another elephant who is in distress or when discovering a corpse. Here, elephant expert Cynthia Moss describes one such encounter in her book *Elephant Memories*:

> They stood around Tina's carcass, touching it gently.... Because it was rocky and the ground was wet, there was no loose dirt; but they tried to dig into it... and when they managed to get a little earth up they sprinkled it over the body. Trista, Tia, and some of the others went off and broke branches from the surrounding low brushes and

> brought them back and placed them on the carcass.... By nightfall they had nearly buried her with branches and earth. Then they stood vigil over her for most of the night and only as dawn was approaching did they reluctantly begin to walk away.

Iain Douglas-Hamilton and his colleagues have shown that elephants also extend this compassion to nonrelatives — to those who aren't genetically related. And elephants display a well-documented fascination with death and bones. Many experts describe seeing these magnificent mammoths become excited and agitated when they come across a dead elephant. Karen McComb, an expert on animal communication and cognition, and her colleagues performed a unique field experiment to study the concern that elephants show for the dead. They presented skulls and other objects to nineteen groups of wild elephants. They discovered that the animals preferred to investigate elephant bones and tusks and could even distinguish elephant skulls from those of other species. Researchers also found that the wild elephants spent twice as much time examining the elephant skulls as they did the buffalo and rhino skulls.

And what, besides love and despair, could possibly be animating the elephants in the following story? Here, Cynthia Moss describes the actions of the same elephant family above after a group member had been shot:

> Teresia and Trista became frantic and knelt down and tried to lift her up. They worked their tusks under her back and under her head. At one point they succeeded in lifting her into a sitting position but her body flopped back down. Her family tried everything to rouse her, kicking and tusking her, and Tullulah even went off and collected a trunkful of grass and tried to stuff it in her mouth.

Howling Wolves

Louis Dorfman, an animal behaviorist at the International Exotic Feline Sanctuary in Boyd, Texas, tells a story of how a wolf he knew well expressed deep grief and gratitude:

> With other wild animals, I have experienced many deep and complex emotions. As an example, I lived with a Canadian timber wolf for fifteen years. When her German shepherd playmate died, she sniffed him, then sat back and gave the most soulful and heart-wrenching howl I've ever heard! It lasted quite a while. She'd never howled in that manner before, nor did she ever again afterwards. She was also quite a female. She would flirt, tease, be as loving and gentle as a lamb, and she was quite sensitive to my moods and would respond appropriately to whatever I was feeling with great care and thought. When she became quite ill, could not even lift her head, and compassion dictated I take her to the veterinarian and say "Good-bye," as I was holding her head in my arms at the last minute while the veterinarian was preparing, she looked deeply into my eyes and, with great effort, lifted her head to lick my face one last time. I will never in my life forget that last effort; a desire to let me know I was doing the right thing and she loved me for it!

Filmmakers Jim and Jamie Dutcher describe the grief and mourning in a wolf pack after the loss of the low-ranking omega female wolf, Motaki, to a mountain lion. The pack lost their spirit and their playfulness. They no longer howled as a group, but rather they "sang alone in a slow mournful cry." They were depressed — tails and heads held low and walking softly and slowly — when they came upon the place where Motaki was killed. They inspected the area and pinned their ears back and dropped their tails, a gesture that usually means submission. It took about six weeks for the pack to return to normal. The Dutchers also tell of a wolf pack in Canada, in which one pack member died and the others wandered about in a figure eight as if searching for her. They also howled long and mournfully.

Eternally Devoted: Llamas Teach a Lesson in Grieving

I'd like to end this section on grief by sharing a story that my friend Betsy Webb told to me. Betsy lives in Homer, Alaska, and has lived with llamas for years; she often goes backpacking with them. Her moving story is an elegant testament to the sentient awareness and emotional depth of animals. Betsy wrote:

> Llamas are gregarious by nature, extremely perceptive, and forge deep bonds with one another. In the pasture, our llamas often feed in the same area, sleep next to each other, and stay close together when they face off an unfamiliar animal or predator. On the trail, they become extremely agitated if they lose sight of each other when one stops to rest and falls behind. They vocalize quite a bit. My favorite is their delicate greeting call, which sounds like a miniature bagpipe exhaling.
>
> When my family moved from Colorado to Alaska, we brought our two Colorado llamas with us. As fate would have it, we inherited two Alaska llamas with our new house and grounds. Each twosome had spent their lives together. At first, the twosomes were a bit standoffish, but in time, they became fast friends and a foursome.
>
> Several years later, the oldest llama, Boone, died quite suddenly at twenty-seven years old. One day, he laid down on his side, too weak to get up. The next day, his life partner, Bridger, died in the same fashion, next to him. It was early spring and the ground was still frozen, so we hired a friend with a backhoe to prepare their grave just across the fence. We carefully hoisted Boone and Bridger over the fence and into the ground, and then covered them. The other pair, Taffy and Pumpernickel, stood by and watched the entire process quietly.
>
> For the next two days, stoic Taffy stood across the fence from the grave and stared at the hole in the ground. She barely moved from the spot. Excitable Pumpernickel stayed in his little barn and wailed for two days. On the third day, they emerged from their grieving and resumed their normal activities.
>
> Did Bridger surrender himself to death following the loss of

his lifelong buddy Boone? And Taffy and Pumpernickel, both very distinct personalities, grieved in their own personal ways. For me, the most moving memory of losing two llamas so close together was experiencing the caring and harmonious llama death and grieving process.

LOVE:

Where Science and Poetry Meet

Love. Has there ever been a more troubling and mysterious emotion? Humans have struggled to understand and define love since the dawn of consciousness, so what possible hope is there that we can understand and define love in animals? And yet, though we don't truly understand love, we do not deny its existence, nor do we deny its power. We experience or witness love every day, in a hundred different forms; indeed, as I note above, grief is but the price of love. Since animals grieve, surely they must feel love too.

Love is perhaps the most complex of all emotions, given its bewildering variety of forms and shadings. On this landscape, where science and poetry meet, we find love that is romantic, parental, filial, and erotic, and we see love express itself as friendship, loyalty, affection, tenderness, devotion, commitment, and compassion.

If I were to hazard a definition, one that we could use to examine animal behavior in search of love, I'd say that love means preferring the close company of another individual, seeking them out, and if necessary protecting and caring for them. It means forming and maintaining strong and close reciprocal social bonds and communicating feelings between loved ones. Not exactly poetry, but it's a start.

There's considerable evidence that many animals are capable of feelings that run the gamut of the varieties of love, and the latest science argues for the existence of love in many different species. The brain machinery of love — the neuroanatomy and neurochemistry that allow us to feel love — is similar or identical to that of numerous other animals. Once again, science is catching up with what our intuitions already tell us, and in the following sections, we will look at love that is romantic (that involves selecting and keeping a mate), maternal (that involves parent-child bonding), and filial (that involves love between siblings or friends).

Love and Marriage

So much research has been done on the mating styles and habits of animals that it's clear that romantic love isn't uniquely human, nor, I should add, are humans role models for marriage, or committed love. How much of this is chemical and how much of this is purely "emotional" is a matter of debate, even regarding human love. But anyone who's lived with a cat or a dog — or watched cows, sheep, or pigs — knows that animals fall in love. And as with all their emotions, their love is as pure and unfiltered as it can be.

In many species, individuals take the time to get to know one another and to reinforce their close bonds. Romantic love can be slow to develop, and mating rituals can take a lot of time and energy. These rituals even sometimes involve physical risk, and sometimes vows need to be renewed. Male marmosets spend a good deal of time figuring out who to mate with. Evidence from functional Magnetic Resonance Imaging (fMRI) studies shows that they make careful decisions and evaluate what they're getting into before they mate. In many canids — that is, members of the dog family, which includes wolves, coyotes, foxes, jackals, and dingoes — males and females who have mated for years still greet one another like they're long-lost friends and court vigorously, even though they've done it before.

And just to be clear, "courtship" is not a euphemism for sex; it describes the same "romantic" dance that you would witness at any high school prom. For example, Bernd Würsig describes the courtship of southern right whales, which he observed off Peninsula Valdis, Argentina. While courting, the male and female whales continuously touch flippers, beginning with a slow caressing motion. Then they roll toward each other, briefly locking both sets of flippers as in a hug, and roll back up, lying side by side. They then swim off, side by side, touching, surfacing, and diving in unison. Würsig says he followed the pair for about an hour, during which they continued to travel together.

Whales are fellow mammals, but there's compelling evidence that fish also make choices about mating. They're not automatons. Researcher Lee Dugatkin observed what he calls "guppy love." Dugatkin discovered that males change their behavior and become bolder in response to a predator when there is a female around, because females find bold males more attractive. Even among fish, it seems like males will risk it all for love.

Helen Fisher, author of *Why We Love*, put forth what she calls an "immodest proposal" concerning the evolution of love: "All these data lead me to believe that animals big and little are biologically driven to prefer, pursue, and possess specific mating partners; there is chemistry to animal attraction. And this chemistry must be the precursor to human love."

The most devoted mates are not necessarily our closest kin, the great apes, or other mammals. More than 90 percent of bird species are monogamous, and many mate for life. Fewer mammals are monogamous, and the nonhuman primates appear comparatively callous when it comes to commitment. Chimpanzee males, for example, don't spend much time courting, mating, or remaining with a female whose young they've fathered. When males aren't needed to provide protection or food for their mates or their offspring, they frequently try to mate with as many females as possible. That sounds like "happy hour" at the watering hole to me.

A Mother's Love

Just as romantic love among animals has been well documented, so too has maternal love. This love is sometimes displayed most dramatically when a child is in trouble; mothers of many species will fight to the death to protect their offspring, and when a child is hurt or killed, they exhibit the deepest feelings of grief and pain. Sea lion mothers, watching their babies being eaten by killer whales, squeal eerily and wail pitifully in anguish over their loss, and dolphins have been observed struggling to save a dead infant.

Mother love couldn't be more primal. In the first known example of an invertebrate caring for its young, Australian leeches, or bloodsuckers, have been shown to be devoted parents. They carry their newborn and nurture their young for up to six weeks after hatching. They also protect their children from predators and carry them to new areas where they'll be safe.

Mother love is found in innumerable species. Killer whales, or orcas, may not be very nice to the animals they eat, but they are good, very loving parents. Baby whales are born ready to swim, and like human children, they are very curious infants. Naomi Rose, who works at the Humane Society of the United States, once watched a large group of orcas along the coast of Vancouver Island in Canada. One day Naomi saw a mother surface without her calf and discovered that the young orca had swum behind her boat. The calf was playing and having a good time exploring his surroundings, but his head was very close to the propeller. In a few minutes, the calf's mother arrived next to the boat, but rather than chase her calf away, she simply kept a close eye on him. She tolerated his curiosity and playful spirit, while remaining watchful for danger. Could it be that this orca mother was trying to negotiate that delicate balance all mothers face: wanting to keep her child safe, but not be overprotective?

Elephants are well known to be very devoted parents, and elephant expert Cynthia Moss tells the following story of a mother's devotion. In late February of one year, Echo, the "beautiful matriarch" of her elephant family, gave birth to a male, Ely, who could not stand up because his front legs were bent. He was born with rigid carpal joints. Echo continually tried to lift Ely by reaching her trunk under and around him. Each time Ely stood, he was able to shuffle around on his knees for a short while, but then he would collapse to the ground.

Eventually, the other clan members left, and Echo and her nine-year-old daughter, Enid, stayed with Ely. Despite the fact that Echo and Enid were hungry and thirsty, they wouldn't leave an exhausted Ely to go to the watering hole. After a great deal of effort, all three elephants were able to reach the watering hole, where Echo and Enid splashed themselves as well as Ely. Echo and Enid then made low rumbling calls to the rest of their family. After three days, Ely's joints loosened, and he finally was able to stand on his own.

But there is more to the story. When Ely was seven years old, he suffered a serious wound from a spear that was embedded about one foot into his back. Although Echo now had another calf, she remained strongly bonded to Ely and would not allow a team of veterinarians to tend to him. When Ely fell down after being tranquilized, Echo and other clan members tried to lift him. Echo, Enid, and another of Echo's daughters, Eliot, remained near Ely despite attempts by the veterinarians to disperse the elephants so that they could help Ely. The elephants refused to leave despite gunshots being fired over their heads. Finally, Ely was treated and survived the injury. Echo's lifelong devotion to Ely has been rewarded, and today Ely is a very healthy twelve years old.

Truly, Love Is Blind

One could argue that attracting a mate and protecting one's offspring are genetically hardwired instincts. What looks like "love" is actually unthinking evolution protecting its investment. There may be some truth to this — the desire to reproduce certainly seems instinctual — but biological needs alone don't explain the wide range of emotions animals display, and they certainly don't explain the stories that follow. In these, animals are seen acting with incredible devotion and care even though there's no biological advantage to be had.

Several years ago, a story appeared about two Jack Russell terriers who were found, filthy and terrified, cowering on the main street of a small town. The dogs were friends, not mates. One was bleeding from both eyes; the other was standing guard, barking and snapping at anyone who approached. They were taken to a veterinarian, who determined that the one terrier had been stabbed: both eyes had to be removed and the lids sewn up. Two days after the operation, Ben, as he had been named, was reunited with Bill in the local animal shelter. From that moment on, Bill acted as Ben's guide dog; with Ben holding on to the scruff of his neck, Bill walked him around the yard until he knew the lay of the land. After a TV crew captured this amazing performance, the two dogs found a marvelous home with an elderly couple who had an old female Jack Russell. With Bill's nudges and tugs, Ben quickly learned to negotiate the little house and garden. They sleep curled up together and behave "rather like a married couple."

Incredibly, this is not the only story of a sighted animal helping a blind animal that I've heard: consider the tale of Annie, a blind mule, and her constant companion and guide, Charlie, a steer. Both were permanent residents of Colorado's Black Forest Animal Sanctuary (BFAS), a nonprofit rescue organization. Annie was nursing a broken shoulder and bound for the slaughterhouse when BFAS volunteers brought her in. She lived at the ranch for more than a year before she met Charlie. Initially, Charlie and Annie were kept in separate pastures, but during one cold spell all the livestock was herded into a single pen for warmth. Charlie hit it off with Annie. He started nuzzling up to her and playing with her. Today, the two are inseparable. Annie used to have a hard time finding the water tank, but Charlie unfailingly leads her to it. She follows him around the pasture, avoiding bumping into the fence, and as with Bill and Ben, they sleep cuddled up together.

As I describe in chapter 1, there are numerous stories of animals of different species who form close social bonds that resemble what we call love. A one-year-old hippopotamus, named Owen by his caretakers, formed a close bond with a century-old male tortoise named Mzee (Swahili for old man) after floods in Kenya (due to a tsunami in 2004) left Owen dehydrated and alone. Owen was found by wildlife rangers near the Indian Ocean and brought to a wildlife sanctuary in Mombasa. Owen now sleeps and eats with his tortoise friend, and the two have remained inseparable, close buddies.

Love Dogs

As we all know, dogs are "man's best friend." Their devotion to humans is undeniable. They can also be best friends to one another. I'd like to end this section on love by sharing the story of two beautiful malamutes, Tika, and her longtime mate, Kobuk, who had raised eight litters of puppies together and now were enjoying their retirement years in the home of Anne Bekoff, who shared their story with me. Kobuk was charming, energetic, and always demanded attention. He'd always let you know when he wanted his belly rubbed or his ears scratched. He also was quite vocal and howled his way into everyone's heart. Tika was quieter and pretty low key. If anyone tried to rub Tika's ears or belly, Kobuk shoved his way in. Tika knew not to eat her food unless it was far away from Kobuk. If Tika happened to get in Kobuk's way when he headed to the door, she usually got knocked over as he charged past her.

Then one day a small lump appeared on Tika's leg. It was diagnosed as a malignant tumor. Overnight Kobuk's behavior changed. He became subdued and wouldn't leave Tika's side. Then Tika had to have her leg amputated and had trouble getting around. Kobuk, clearly worried about her, stopped shoving her aside and stopped caring if she was allowed to get on the bed without him.

About two weeks after Tika's surgery, Kobuk woke Anne in the middle of the night the way he did when he really needed to go outside. Tika was in another room, and Kobuk ran over to her. Anne got Tika up and took both dogs outside, but the dogs just lay down on the grass. Tika was whining softly, and Anne saw that Tika's belly was huge and swollen. Anne realized that Tika was going into shock, so she rushed her to the emergency animal clinic in Boulder. The veterinarian operated on her and was able to save her life.

If Kobuk hadn't fetched Anne, Tika almost certainly would have died. Tika recovered, and as her health grew after the amputation and operation, Kobuk became the bossy dog he'd always been, even as Tika walked around on three legs. But Anne had witnessed their true relationship. Kobuk and Tika, a true old married couple, would always be there for each other, even if their personalities would never change. They were love dogs doing for each other what needed to be done.

In our dealings with them, we would be wise to follow our animal friends' example. It is certainly my fervent hope that one day we will.

EMBARRASSMENT:

Can a Monkey Blush?

Do animals ever feel embarrassed? It may seem like a silly question, but the ability to be embarrassed might be one sign of a sentient, self-aware being. If you have no sense of self, then who cares who's looking, right?

Embarrassment is difficult to observe; by definition it's a feeling that one tries to hide. But Jane Goodall believes she has observed what could be called embarrassment in chimpanzees. Fifi was a female chimpanzee who Jane knew for more than forty years (she was the daughter of an equally famous female, Flo). When Fifi's oldest child, Freud, was five and a half years old, his uncle, Fifi's brother Figan, was the alpha male of their chimpanzee community. Freud always followed Figan; he hero-worshipped the big male. Once, as Fifi groomed Figan, Freud climbed up the thin stem of a wild plantain. When he reached the leafy crown, he began swaying wildly back and forth. Had he been a human child, we would have said he was showing off. Suddenly the stem broke and Freud tumbled into the long grass. He was not hurt. He landed close to Jane, and as his head emerged from the grass, she saw him look over at Figan — had he noticed? If he had, he paid no attention but went on grooming. Freud very quietly climbed another tree and began to feed.

Harvard University psychologist Marc Hauser observed what could be called embarrassment in a male rhesus monkey. After mating with a female, the male strutted away and accidentally fell into a ditch. He stood up and quickly looked around. After sensing that no other monkeys saw him tumble, he marched off, back high, head and tail up, as if nothing had happened.

Of course, two anecdotes, however intriguing, aren't proof. Once again, comparative research in neurobiology, endocrinology, and ethology is needed to learn more about the subjective nature of embarrassment. If we study the neural and hormonal correlates of embarrassment in humans and see similar patterns in animals (as we've done for joy), then we're on safe ground claiming that animals are capable of experiencing embarrassment. These anecdotes do raise the possibility, and there's no good reason to think animals can't.

RED IN TOOTH AND CLAW:
Anger, Aggression, and Revenge

As with joy and fear, there's no question that animals can get angry in the same ways that humans can get angry. We share common neurochemicals (such as serotonin and testosterone) and brain structures (such as the hypothalamus) that are important in the expression and feeling of anger, aggression, and revenge. It's easy to identify anger and aggression as well, for it often appears raw and unfiltered.

Nevertheless, expressions of anger don't always lead to actual violence and injury. Male giraffes will often "neck" each other when they are upset. Necking involves the giraffes walking toward each other, standing side by side, and each gently grazing the other's neck with his horns. Biologist Anne Dagg, who studied giraffes for more than twenty years, never saw necking lead to a real fight.

Even octopuses seem to get angry. According to researcher Roland Anderson, their pearly white skin turns red when they are agitated, and if you ever see a red octopus, it's likely angry and should be avoided.

Birds, monogamous mates that they are, can display tremendous anger and aggression. Researcher Irene Pepperberg studied Alex, an extremely smart gray parrot, for decades and noted that when something didn't happen as Alex expected, he got very angry. For instance, most of the time Alex was easy to get along with — his eyes were wide open, his feathers flat, and his head up. But if Alex was fed a pellet of bird food instead of a cashew, which he much preferred, he would narrow his eyes, puff up his feathers, and lower his head, all of which indicated his displeasure.

Birds are also well known for their sibling conflicts. While siblings can be friends — they will protect one another and cooperate against a common enemy — they will also evict one another from the safety of a nest, steal food from one another (even in times of plenty), and sometimes kill one another (which is called siblicide). In American pelicans, sibling fighting is common, and fights to the death occur in black eagles, cattle egrets, great blue herons, and Mexican blue-footed boobies. Usually, the oldest and largest siblings start fights. In one study of black eagles, the older chick relentlessly pursued his younger sibling and pecked him more than fifteen hundred times during thirty-eight attacks. The senior chick gained fifty grams during this period, whereas the younger chick lost eighteen grams.

Siblicide is obviously driven by the competition to survive, but that makes it no less emotional for the combatants. There are actually fewer good examples of siblicide in mammals because much rivalry occurs in dens and cannot be seen. But it is documented in both Galapagos fur seals and spotted hyenas. In general, same-sex aggression is more common and heated than aggression between the sexes.

An Outcast among Hyenas

Spotted hyenas are African carnivores who live in clans. When they get angry, they usually work out their differences without fighting. If one hyena is bothered by one of its clan mates, all it has to do is approach the other hyena or wave its head toward the other hyena. Usually, the other hyena walks away. If he or she doesn't, then there may be a chase. Biting does not occur very often and only when the hyenas are really mad at each other.

Researchers Kay Holekamp and Laura Smale studied spotted hyenas in Kenya, and they saw intense aggression only once, when an adult female hyena named Little Gullwing attempted to rejoin her clan after being away for a year.

Little Gullwing was clearly nervous about rejoining her friends. She approached them with her ears flattened against her head, her tail between her legs, and wearing a calming grin. As she approached, she bobbed her head up and down and side to side, indicating submission.

But her old friends didn't accept her. They raised their tails and put their ears forward while the hair on their backs stood up. They became excited and agitated at Little Gullwing's return. In response Little Gullwing dropped to the ground and crawled toward the other hyenas. Crawling usually stops other hyenas from being aggressive, but this time it didn't work. Little Gullwing's clan treated her as they would a trespasser from another clan, and they drove her away.

Nasty Nick: Stories of a Mean and Pissy Baboon

Nick, an olive baboon, was an adolescent when he joined what was known as the "Forest Troop" in the southeast corner of Masai Mara National Reserve in Kenya, and even then you could almost see contempt on his face. Or so says world-famous Stanford professor Robert Sapolsky, who described Nick in *A Primate's Memoirs*. Sapolsky writes that Nick dominated his age group, and "he was confident, unflinching, and played dirty." One time, Nick trounced another baboon named Reuben in a fight, and afterward Rueben "stuck his ass up in the air" — which is a sign of submission, giving up. Nick went over as if to examine his bottom and then slashed him with his canines. Sapolsky is known for speaking eloquently and plainly about animal behavior, whether it sounds like anthropomorphizing or not, and he is equally blunt about Nick:

> The guy simply wasn't nice.... He harassed the females, swatted at kids, bullied ancient Gums and Limp. On one memorable day, he took exception to something that poor nervous Ruth had done and chased her up a tree. Typically, at this point, the female takes advantage of one of those rare instances when it pays to be smaller than the males — she goes to the farthest end of a flimsy branch and hangs on for dear life, depending on the fact that the heavier male can't crawl out to where she is and bite her. And, typically, the male, thwarted, positions himself to at least trap the female, keeping her screaming on the precarious branch until he gets bored. So Ruth gallops up the tree, Nick after her, and Ruth leaps out to a safe edge. Nick promptly climbs onto a stronger, thicker branch directly above her. And then urinates on her head.

Nick was a bully and a competitive Darwinian nightmare, but he was also infuriatingly smart. In another episode, Sapolsky had darted Reuben with a sedative as part of an experiment in behavioral physiology. After darting, a baboon becomes unconscious, and Sapolsky and his field team can handle him, in this case to determine the relationship between the individual's dominance rank, personality, and physiology. However, as Reuben was slowly going under, Nick approached. Reuben lifted his head, saw Nick, and gave him a fear grimace. Then Nick placed his hand on Reuben's shoulder and the other on his haunch, leaned back, and bellowed a "wahoo" call. After holding this pose, Nick marched back into the underbrush. "I couldn't believe it" Sapolsky writes, "That bastard had just taken credit for my darting."

This is not to say that anger is always a function of survival competition or plain meanness. For instance, in Saudi Arabia, a man hit and killed a baboon with his car. Afterward, the baboon's troop lay in waiting for three days by the side of the road until the same driver appeared again. As the driver passed the troop, one baboon screamed, and then all the baboons threw stones at the car and tore out its windshield.

And Please, Don't Tease the Chimpanzee

Finally, here is another cautionary tale. Ron Schusterman, a marine biologist at the University of California–Santa Cruz, loves to tell the story of Franz, a young male chimpanzee who was kept in a lab and known to be a feces thrower. Ron's friend Larry was one of Franz's favorite targets. One day, Larry noticed that Franz's cage had been cleaned up, and so he teased Franz: "You can't get me — na na na na na." Franz stared at Larry while he was being taunted, and when Larry finished, Franz regurgitated some partially digested food he had been fed a few minutes earlier and threw it at Larry, splattering him across the front. Franz then ran around in a victory dance.

ARE THERE AUTISTIC COYOTES AND BIPOLAR WOLVES?

Because it's usually ignored, I want to pose a final question in this chapter: if animals feel many, if not most, of the emotions humans feel, can they also become mentally impaired? While we see emotions being freely and openly expressed in a wide variety of species, often there are individuals who seem to be "out of it." For example, on occasion I've seen a young animal who just doesn't seem to get it, an individual who just doesn't know how to play. I remember a coyote pup named Harry who didn't respond to play signals by playing, as did most of his littermates. Harry also didn't use play bows very often and just didn't seem to have a clue about how to initiate play, or even how to play if he got to do it at all. For a long time I simply chalked it up to individual variation, figuring that since behavior among members of the same species can vary, Harry wasn't all that surprising.

But I was recently asked if there were autistic animals, and I thought about Harry and realized I wasn't sure. Because there are autistic humans, there likely are nonhuman animals who suffer from what might be called autism. Perhaps Harry suffered from coyote autism. Simon Baron-Cohen has made great strides in learning about human autism using ethological studies, and ethologist Niko Tinbergen eventually turned his attention to the study of autism, so there may indeed be a useful connection.

I remember other animals. There was another coyote, a large male named Joe, who seemed to go all over the place. He'd often seem to be sulking and moping around for no obvious reason and then instantaneously run around as if he were happy, seemingly without a care in the world. Then there was Lucy, a young wolf who behaved similarly to Joe. Some days Lucy behaved "normally," like a typical wolf, whereas on others she was either really wired or really down. Other colleagues have also remarked that on occasion one of the animals they're watching seems to be very unusual. But we never thought to call the out-of-the-ordinary individuals autistic or bipolar.

Perhaps, to be consistent with arguments about evolutionary continuity and emotions, this would not be out of order. As I note above, experienced ethologists and psychologists now believe that elephants hurt like us and heal from psychological trauma like us and suffer from posttraumatic stress disorder. (They have a huge hippocampus, a brain structure in the limbic system that's important in processing emotions.) Then how far do we need to stretch to include autistic and bipolar animals? Many different psychological disorders have been diagnosed in dogs, so there's no reason why this couldn't be true for their wild relatives and other creatures.

Now let's look at an even more intriguing possibility: that animals possess moral sensibilities, and that these are the evolutionary precursors of our own moral behavior.

CHAPTER 4

Wild Justice, Empathy, and Fair Play: Finding Honor among Beasts

Those communities which included the greatest number of the most sympathetic members would flourish best and rear the greatest number of offspring.

— CHARLES DARWIN, *THE DESCENT OF MAN AND SELECTION IN RELATION TO SEX*

I've long been interested in play behavior. This might sound like a frivolous field of study — a number of my colleagues certainly told me so when I first started — but after years of examining videotapes of playing dogs, coyotes, and wolves and trying to understand why animals play the way they do, I have been led to ask a series of big and ultimately surprising questions: Do animals play fair? Do they negotiate agreements to play (as opposed to fighting or mating), and do those agreements require cooperating, forgiving, apologizing, and admitting when they're wrong, as well as trusting others? Are animals honest? If one breaks their agreement, do they consider that wrong? Are there consequences for doing something wrong? If animals demonstrate a dislike for getting the short end of the stick or being short-changed, does that indicate that animals have a sense of justice, of right and wrong, good and bad —

does that mean, in other words, that animals are moral beings? And if animals can be shown to display a sense of justice along with a wide range of cognitive and emotional capacities, including empathy and reciprocity, does that make the differences between humans and all other animals a matter of degree rather than kind?

Finally, if all this is true, then is morality in fact an evolved trait? Does "being fair" mean being more fit — does being more virtuous improve an individual's reproductive fitness, while being less virtuous harm it? To put it anther way, do nice guys, gals, and their genes last longest? Do the nicest survive best?

These are indeed big, complicated, difficult questions, but mounting evidence points straight to the conclusion that there is "honor among beasts." While much of the research that's been aired widely deals with nonhuman primates, especially the work of Frans de Waal and his colleagues at Emory University in Atlanta, Georgia, there are also compelling data from studies on social carnivores that support the claim that moral behavior is more widespread among animals than previously thought. In *Primates and Philosophers: How Morality Evolved*, de Waal argues that human morality is on a continuum with animal sociality, though he isn't sure that animals are moral beings. However, he doesn't consider social play behavior.

Based on my long-term detailed studies of play in social carnivores — including wolves, coyotes, red foxes, and domestic dogs — I believe we can make the stronger claim that some animals might be moral beings. Other ethologists (such as Nobel laureate Niko Tinbergen and the well-known field biologist George Schaller) certainly stress that we might learn more about the evolution of human behavior from studies of social carnivores than from studies of other primates because the social behavior and social organization of many carnivores resemble that of early hominids in a number of important ways (divisions of labor, food sharing, care of young, and intrasexual and intersexual dominance hierarchies). Given this, social carnivores may hold the key for unlocking the nuances of animal morality.

So how does play figure into discussions of morality? To begin with, when animals play, there are rules of engagement that must be followed, and when these break down, play suffers. Animal play appears to rely on the universal human value of the Golden Rule — do unto others as you would have them do unto you. Following this requires empathy (feeling another's feelings) and implies reciprocity (getting paid back for favors assuming that others follow the same rule). Further, in the social arena, animals who don't play well don't seem to do as well as those who do play. Darwin might very well have been right when he speculated that more sympathetic individuals have more reproductive success — they survive better. By the end of this chapter, I propose that this means we should make another paradigm shift in how we understand animals and ourselves. "Survival of the fittest" has always been used to refer to the most successful *competitor*, but in fact *cooperation* may be of equal or more importance. It is likely that for any species individual survival requires both to some degree, while for social species (as opposed to asocial species) the balance may shift significantly, with the most cooperative individuals most often "winning" the evolutionary race.

We still need to learn a great deal about the importance of cooperative behavior and its relationship to wild justice. Indeed, it's only in the past decade that discussing morality in animals hasn't automatically been met with a skeptical raised eyebrow and a disdainful laugh. Traditionally, morality has been the exclusive right of humans, even sometimes the very definition of our humanness, and some scientists and others still vehemently resist the idea that we might actually share this quality with other beings. Yet more and more biologists, neuroscientists, philosophers, and ethologists are beginning to think that morality may be a broadly adaptive strategy that has evolved in many species. I'm not saying animal moral behavior is the same as human moral behavior. Rather, my proposal is that the phenomenon to which "morality" refers is a wide-ranging biological necessity for social living. Just as emotions are a gift of our ancestors, so too are the basic ingredients of morality: namely, cooperation, empathy, fairness, justice, and trust.

PHILOSOPHICAL QUESTIONS:

Distinguishing Morals and Ethics

Before going any further, it's important to make clear what I'm not proposing. Philosophers sometimes make a distinction between morals and ethics. *Ethics* is the philosophical study of moral beliefs and behaviors (equivalent to "moral philosophy"). Ethics suggests the contemplative study of subtle questions of rightness or fairness. Ethics is wondering why fairness exists, why one action is considered "fair" and another isn't. Here, I'm arguing that some animals have moral codes of behavior, but not that animals have ethics. They may sit around, paw to chin, regarding the world like Rodin's *Thinker*, but I don't think they are contemplating "why good is good." As far as we know this is a distinctively human phenomenon.

The word *moral* was first coined in the fourteenth century as an extension of the Latin *mos*, "custom." Mos described the proper behavior of a person in society, and referred especially to one's manners. In its most basic form, morality can be thought of as "prosocial" behavior — behavior aimed at promoting (or at least not diminishing) the welfare of others. Morality is an essentially *social* phenomenon: it arises in the interactions between and among individuals, and it exists as a kind of webbing or fabric that holds together a complicated tapestry of social relationships. The word *morality* has since become shorthand for knowing the difference between right and wrong, between being good and being bad.

In the context of animals, morality refers to a wide-ranging suite of social behaviors; it is an internalized set of rules for how to act within a community. Moral behavior includes (but may not be limited to) cooperation, reciprocity, empathy, and helping. Morality has emotional, or affective, components, and it also has cognitive components. My colleague Jessica Pierce sees human morality experienced as, and also enforced through, a number of regulating mechanisms: anger, indignation, guilt, conscience, shame, reputation, ostracism, retribution, joy, love, disgust, and desire. More research needs to be done on how animals enforce and regulate morality.

DEFINING "FAIRNESS"

Animals exhibit fairness during play, and they react negatively to unfair behavior. In this context, "fairness" has to do with an individual's specific social expectations and not some universally defined standard of right and wrong. If I expect a friend to play with me and he acts in an aggressive manner — dominating or hitting me rather than cooperating and "playing" — then I will feel I am being treated unfairly because of a lapse in social etiquette. We have found, by studying the details and dynamics of social play behavior in animals, that animals exhibit a similar sense of fairness. For instance, one way we know that animals have social expectations is that they show surprise when things don't go "right" during play, and only further communication keeps play going. For example, during play when a dog becomes too assertive, too aggressive, or tries to mate, the other dog may cock her head from side to side and squint, as if she's wondering what went "wrong." For a moment, the violation of trust stops play, and play continues only if the playmate "apologizes" by indicating through gestures, such as a play bow, his intention to keep playing.

Social play is thus based on a "foundation of fairness." Play occurs only if animals agree to cooperate, if they have no other agenda but to play, and if, for the time they are playing, they put aside or neutralize any inequalities in physical size and social rank. As we will see, large and small animals can play together, and high- and low-ranking individuals can play together, but not if one of them takes advantage of its superior strength or status.

It may turn out that play is a unique category of behavior in that inequalities are tolerated more so than in other social contexts. Play can't occur if the individuals choose not to engage in the activity, and the equality or fairness needed for play to continue makes it different from other forms of cooperative behavior (such as hunting and caregiving). Play is perhaps uniquely egalitarian. And if we define justice or morality as a set of social rules and expectations that neutralize differences among individuals in an effort to maintain group harmony, then that's exactly what we find in animals when they play.

MORALITY IN ANIMALS: They Have It Too

People who resist the idea of "moral animals" tend to hold one of two opposing beliefs: either it's impossible because humans are clearly the only beings blessed with such virtues, or it's impossible because all animals, including humans, are obviously inherently immoral and amoral. I'd like to quickly address both these reactions, since they can keep us from having an open mind and seeing animals as they actually are.

Those who would put humans on a pedestal above all other creatures feel threatened by the possibility of morality in animals, since it seems to threaten the special and unique status of humans. This idea that humans are the most virtuous creatures usually comes from religion, so to say animals can be moral is sometimes perceived as a threat against some deeply held religious beliefs. But it's not. This isn't an either-or situation: either humans are special or no one is special. Both can be true: humans have ethics and spiritual awareness, *and* animals display moral codes of behavior. The only thing that is threatened by the proposition that animals are moral beings is the belief that morality alone defines our "human nature." To me, what sets us apart is our ability to conceive of a "human nature." As I say above, dogs are dogs, and they probably don't ponder their "dogness" — but they do know when another dog breaks their trust, and they may shame that dog or avoid him in the future. In fact, it makes good evolutionary sense to assume that morality evolved in other animals, and it wouldn't be the first time that a trait used to separate humans from other animals actually brought them closer together. For instance, before Jane Goodall's groundbreaking discovery, it was assumed that tool use was uniquely human, but now we know that many primates as well as corvids and other animals fashion and use tools.

Then there are the pessimists. At a social hour at a meeting of the Animal Behavior Society, one of my esteemed colleagues heard me talking about animal morality and walked away scratching his head thinking I'd had too much beer. He was especially concerned because of the abundance of *immoral* behavior that humans display daily. "So," he exclaimed, "how can you talk about morality in animals when we're so #&$#^$%#* amoral?"

On one level, he's right: humans can be selfish, unfair, and uncaring, and their moral codes can sometimes be self-servingly hypocritical. Just take a cursory glance at the front page of the newspaper: the murder of a family during a robbery is considered unacceptable, but not so killing in self-defense or as part of a distant, "justified" war. Humans can lie, steal, and cheat, and they can justify their actions so they never feel "wrong." At times, indeed, it can be hard to imagine how anyone could consider humans morally "above" any other animal beings.

However, it is just as easy to find examples of human kindness, compassion, and generosity. Humans are capable of both virtuous and less-than-virtuous behavior, just as nonhuman animals show themselves capable of fair and unfair behavior. I'm not proposing that animals are necessarily *more* virtuous than humans, but simply that many species, to varying degrees, have social standards for behavior. Individuals may break their standards or uphold them, but they all understand them, and they understand that there are social consequences based on what they do. Neither am I proposing that dog morality is the same as chimpanzee morality, or that chimpanzee morality is the same as human morality, and so on, but I do believe we can find the evolutionary roots of what we call human morality by carefully studying the behavior of other animals.

JEROME AND FERD:

Two Dogs at Play

A few years ago one of my students, Josh, called me and, with much excitement in his voice, told me the following story of watching his 120-pound malamute, Jerome, engaged in play:

> I saw the most amazing thing today at Mount Sanitas. Jerome wanted to play with a strange dog named Ferd who was about a quarter his size. Jerome bowed, barked, wagged his tail, rolled over on his back, leapt up, and bowed again, all to no avail. Ferd just stood there with surprising indifference. But about a minute later, while Jerome was sniffing a bush where a large mutt had just peed, Ferd strolled over and launched onto Jerome's neck, and bit him hard and was sort of hanging in midair, legs off the ground. I thought, this is it; Jerome will kill this little monster.
>
> And you know what? Jerome shrugged Ferd off like a fly on his back, turned around and bowed, and then took the little guy's head into his mouth and gently mouthed him. They then played for about half an hour, during which Jerome never ever was very assertive or unfair. He'd bite Ferd softly, roll over, paw at his friend's face, and swat him lightly. Then when things got rough, and Ferd backed off with his tail down and cocking his head from side to side — trying to figure out if he was a goner — Jerome would bow again and they'd play some more. Jerome seemed to know that he had to be nice and fair in order to play with his little buddy. Ferd knew what Jerome wanted,

and Jerome knew what Ferd wanted, and they worked together to get it. Man, dogs are smart. I couldn't believe it.

Josh was a good student. He understood the "language" of animal play (which I describe further below), and so he was able to "read" this encounter and all of its internal communications. However, I'm willing to guess that anyone watching these two mismatched dogs would have been able to tell, after a few minutes, that they were playing and not fighting — just as we can tell at a distance whether two boys who are wrestling really mean to hurt each other or whether they are just kidding around. This is because, when animals play, they must *agree* to play. They must cooperate and behave fairly, and the language of cooperation is easy to recognize. Further, when cooperation and fairness break down, play not only stops, it becomes impossible. *Uncooperative play* is an oxymoron, and that is a large reason why play is such a clear window into the moral lives of animals.

WHAT IS PLAY?

Most of my research on play has involved domestic dogs and their wild relatives, coyotes and wolves (that is, canids, or members of the dog family), so while I focus on the animals I know best in this chapter, there are ample examples from other animals that support my views on play and social morality. Young cats, chimpanzees, bears, and rats, to name only a few, love to play to exhaustion. Even as I'm writing this at six o'-clock on a cool August morning, two red foxes are playing outside my office. They do this almost every day. One invites the other to play by bowing, the other responds, and then they wrestle, rear up on their hind legs and scream and box, chase one another, rest, and play some more. If one bites the other too hard, there's a brief pause during which they look at each other to make sure all is okay — that this is still play — and then resume romping. They're negotiating with each other to maintain the rules of fair play. So long as they keep negotiating, they feel comfortable playing very vigorously because they share a common goal and know that neither will try to beat up the other.

I think of play as being characterized by what I call the "Five S's of Play": its Spirit, Symmetry, Synchrony, Sacredness, and Soulfulness. The Spirit of play is laid bare for all to see as animals wildly run about, wrestle, and knock one another over. The Symmetry and Synchrony of play is reflected in the harmony of the mutual agreements to trust one another — individuals share intentions to cooperate with one another to prevent play from spilling over into fighting. This trust is Sacred. Finally, there's deepness to play, for animals become so completely immersed in it that I like to say they *are* the play. Play is thus a Soulful activity, an expression of the essence of an individual's being.

There's also incredible freedom and creativity in the flow of play. This is easy to see and amazing to watch. I refer to this as the "Six F's of Play": its Flexibility, Freedom, Friendship, Frolic, Fun, and Flow. As they run about, jump on one another, somersault, and bite one another, animals re-create a mind-boggling array of scenarios and social behaviors. It's difficult to believe that when animals are deep into play they can actually keep track of what they are doing, but they can. It's possible that animals are "practicing" and "rehearsing" important behaviors that will help them to survive. As animals play, it's not unusual to see known mating behaviors intermixed in highly variable kaleidoscopic sequences along with actions that are used during fighting, looking for prey, and avoiding becoming someone else's dinner. In no other activity but play do you see all of these attributes and behaviors occurring together.

FUN, FUN, FUN:
Why Animals Play

Animals love to play because play is fun, and fun is its own very powerful reward. Dogs and other animals seek out play relentlessly, and it's very difficult to get them to stop; normal animals don't usually intentionally seek out activities they don't enjoy. The joy associated with play is so strong that it outweighs the possible risks, such as injury, depletion of energy and therefore compromised growth, and death by a perceptive predator. Young animals know how to play from the get-go, and when they don't, we take that as a sign there's possibly something wrong.

When animals play we can feel their deep joy. Play is contagious, and other animals feel the joy and glee as well. Research on mirror neurons (which I describe in chapter 5) supports the notion that individuals can feel the emotions of others, and this likely is the reason that an atmosphere of play spreads rapidly among animals in a group. In her book *On Talking Terms with Dogs*, Norwegian dog trainer Turgid Rugaas refers to play signals as "calming signals." Animals typically play only when they're relaxed, so the inherent joy and serenity in play often spreads to anyone who is watching.

What we can see with our eyes is also being borne out by scientific research. Studies of brain chemistry in rats support the idea that play is pleasurable and fun. Renowned neurobiologist Jaak Panksepp discovered a close association between opiates and play in rats — an increase in opioid activity facilitates playfulness. Opioids may enhance the pleasures and rewards associated with playing. If this is true in rats, and we already know it's true in humans, then there's little reason to believe that the neurochemical basis of play-inspired joy in dogs, cats, horses, and bears would differ substantially.

Indeed, as we've already seen, animals and humans share many of the same emotions and same chemicals that play a role in the experience and expressions of emotions such as joy and pleasure. Recent research has also shown that when people are cooperating and being fair to one another, it feels good. Since play is dependent on cooperation and fairness, this may be another reason animals love to play. James Rilling and his colleagues have used functional Magnetic Resonance Imaging (fMRI) on humans to show that the brain's pleasure centers are strongly activated when people cooperate with one another. This important research shows that there's a strong neural basis for human cooperation: that it feels good to cooperate, that being nice in social interactions is rewarding. Also, researchers have identified a "trust center" in human brains called the caudate nucleus. Activity in the caudate nucleus is greatest when generosity is repaid with generosity. There's every reason to believe that the brains of animals share this trust center with us. In short, research is showing that we might actually be wired to be nice to one another.

If being nice feels good, then that's a good reason for being nice. It's also a good way for a pattern of behavior to evolve and to remain in an animal's arsenal.

IT BEGINS WITH A BOW:
How Animals Play

We know that birds and many other species engage in social play, but as yet there are too few data from which to draw detailed conclusions about the nature of their play. But in my studies of dogs and other canids, I've learned that they use specific play signals to initiate and to maintain social play. Play is a voluntary activity, and it can't occur if individuals don't agree.

How do animals tell one another "I want to play with you"? Play frequently begins with a bow (which I describe in chapter 2), and bowing is repeated during play sequences so as to insure that play doesn't slip into something else, like fighting or mating. After each individual agrees to play, there are on-going, rapid, and subtle exchanges of information so that their cooperative agreement can be fine-tuned and negotiated on the run, so that the activity remains playful. It's important for players to express and to share their intentions to play.

As I've noted, when animals play they often use actions, such as predatory behavior, antipredatory behavior, and mating that are also carried out in other contexts. Because there's a chance that various behavior patterns that are performed during ongoing social play can be misinterpreted as being real aggression or mating, individuals use a bow to tell one another such messages as "I want to play," "This is still play no matter what I am going to do to you," and "This is still play regardless of what I just did to you."

In order to learn the dynamics of play, it's essential to pay attention to subtle details that can be lost or go unnoticed when, for instance, we are simply watching dogs in the park. Dogs and other animals keep close track of what's happening, so we need to also. My studies of play are based on careful observation and meticulous analyses of videotape. I watch tapes one frame at a time to see what the animals are doing and how they exchange information about their intentions and desires during play. This can be tedious work, and indeed, some of my students who were excited about studying dog play had second thoughts after seeing what it entailed.

After many years of study, I've discovered that the "bow" isn't used randomly but with a purpose. For example, biting accompanied by rapid side-to-side shaking of the head is performed during serious aggressive and predatory encounters, and it can easily be misinterpreted if its meaning isn't modified by a bow. I was surprised to learn that bows are used not only right at the beginning of play to tell another dog "I want to play with you," but also right before biting, accompanied by rapid side-to-side head shaking, as if to say, "I'm going to bite you hard but it's still in play." Bows are also used right after vigorous biting, as if to say, "I'm sorry I just bit you so hard, but it was play." Bows serve as punctuation, an exclamation point, to call attention to what the dog wants.

Infant dogs and their wild relatives rapidly learn how to play fairly using play markers such as the bow, and their response to play bows seems to be innate. Pigs use play markers such as bouncy running and head twisting to communicate their intentions to play. Jessica Flack and her colleagues discovered that juvenile chimpanzees will increase the use of signals to prevent the termination of play by the mothers of their younger play partners. Researchers who study the activity always note that play is highly cooperative. I can't stress enough how important it is that play is carefully negotiated, that it is fine-tuned on the run so that the play mood is maintained. There are social rules that must be followed.

Across many different species there's little evidence that play signals are used to deceive others. Play signals are honest signals, and only very rarely are they used to hide aggressive intentions. Animals almost never say, "I want to play with you" and then, when the other animal is vulnerable, engage in a real attack. This is most likely because there are sanctions for lying. For example, I discovered that coyotes who bow and then attack are unlikely to be chosen as play partners, and they also have difficulty getting others to play. My field studies also have shown that this makes them more likely to leave their group, and this can lower their reproductive fitness.

It's simple: If a dog wants to play, he must ask first by bowing. If the other dog doesn't return the bow, she doesn't want to play, and the first dog must move on.

Other Play Markers: Role-Reversing and Self-Handicapping

The bow isn't the only signal used during social play; two other important ones are role-reversing and self-handicapping. Role-reversing and self-handicapping reduce inequalities in size and dominance rank between players, and they promote the reciprocity and cooperation that's needed for play to occur.

Self-handicapping (or "play inhibition") happens when an individual performs a behavior pattern that might compromise her outside of play. For example, a coyote might decide not to bite her play partner as hard as she can, or she might not play as vigorously as she can. Inhibiting the intensity of a bite during play helps to maintain the play mood. I once picked up a twenty-two-day-old coyote only to have him bite through my thumb with his needle-sharp teeth. His bite drew blood and it really hurt. The fur of young coyotes is very thin, and as I found out, an intense bite results in much pain to the recipient, as evidenced by the high-pitched squeals (the coyotes', not mine!). An intense bite is a play-stopper. In adult wolves, a bite can generate as much as fifteen hundred pounds of pressure per square inch, so there's a good reason to inhibit its force. I once foolishly tried to show a captive adult male wolf, Lupey, where his food was by pointing toward it, and he immediately showed me that he knew where it was by clasping his mouth over my extended forearm and squeezing ever so gently. I wore Lupey's teeth marks for two weeks, but he didn't break skin; we may not have been "playing," but he inhibited his bite anyway. With domestic dogs, one of the great advantages of making sure puppies play with other puppies is that they learn bite inhibition and will most likely never harm another.

Red-necked wallabies, kangaroos of a kind, engage in self-handicapping as well. Biologist Duncan Watson and his colleagues found that these playful creatures adjust their play to the age of their partner. When a partner is younger, the older animal adopts a defensive, flat-footed posture, and pawing rather than sparring occurs. Also, the older player is more tolerant of its partner's tactics and takes the initiative in prolonging interactions.

Fairness and trust are important in the dynamics of playful interactions in rats as well. Psychologist Sergio Pellis discovered that sequences of rat play consist of individuals assessing and monitoring one another and then fine-tuning and changing their own behavior to maintain the play mood. When the rules of play are violated, when fairness breaks down, so does play.

Role-reversing happens when a dominant animal performs an action during play that wouldn't normally occur during real aggression. For example, a dominant wolf might never roll over on his back during fighting, but he will do so while playing. In some instances role-reversing and self-handicapping occur together — a dominant wolf might roll over while playing with a subordinate dog and at the same time inhibit the intensity of a bite. Self-handicapping and role-reversing, along with play invitation signals, serve to communicate an individual's intention to play, and they are important in maintaining fair play.

FAIR IS GOOD:
The Benefits of Play

Play isn't an idle waste of time. Play is essential for an individual's mental and physical well-being. Play is brain food because it provides important nourishment for brain growth; it actually helps to rewire the brain, increasing the connections between neurons in the cerebral cortex. Play also hones cognitive skills, including logical reasoning and behavioral flexibility — the ability to make appropriate choices in changing and unpredictable environments.

But some of the most important benefits of play are social — play helps the individual and the group to get along together. Social play relies on, and also teaches, trust, cooperation, niceness, fairness, forgiveness, and humility. Dogs and their relatives aren't alone in the tactics they use in play. Recent research on nonhuman primates has shown that punishment and apology play important roles in maintaining cooperation.

Why do animals carefully use play signals? Why do they engage in self-handicapping and role-reversing? It's plausible to argue that during social play, immature individuals learn ground rules about what behavior patterns are acceptable to others — how hard they can bite, how roughly they can interact — and how to resolve conflicts in a situation that is safe, enjoyable, and nonthreatening. This is similar to the reasoning behind why human children are encouraged to play organized sports: it teaches them how to behave, how to cooperate and resolve conflicts in a setting where the stakes are not high. Through their behavior, animals show us that they place a premium on playing fairly and trusting others to do so. There are codes of social conduct that regulate actions that are and aren't permissible. What could be a better atmosphere in which to learn about the social skills underlying fairness and cooperation than during social play, where there are few penalties for transgressions? It's also possible that individuals might generalize codes of conduct learned while playing with specific individuals to other group members and to different situations, such as sharing food, defending resources, grooming, and giving care.

Play is not only fun. It's a useful behavior. And studies of play indicate that animals actively cultivate a sense of fairness and cooperation by playing. This becomes even clearer in instances where play breaks down.

GETTING A BAD REPUTATION:
The Costs of Breaking Trust

When animals are not having fun, animals won't play. Animals who don't play often can't interact with others because they don't know how to tell their friends what they want and they can't understand what their friends want. They're not socialized. They can't function as card-carrying members of their own species because they haven't learned how to communicate with others. The consequences of the inability to play well start small but possibly grow quite large.

For instance, dogs don't tolerate noncooperative cheaters, who may be avoided or chased from play groups. When a dog's sense of fairness is violated, there are consequences. While studying dog play on a beach in San Diego, California, for her doctoral dissertation in cognitive science, Alexandra Horowitz observed a dog she called Up-ears enter into a play group and interrupt the play of two other dogs, Blackie and Roxy. Up-ears was chased out of the group, and when she returned, Blackie and Roxy stopped playing and looked off toward a distant sound. In a fooling behavior, Roxy began moving in the direction of the sound, and Up-ears ran off following their line of sight. Having gotten rid of Up-ears, Roxy and Blackie immediately began playing once again.

Of much more importance to biologists, however, is how differences in the performance of a given behavior, such as play, influence an individual's reproductive success. Do differences in play and variations in fair play affect an individual's reproductive fitness? If we want to know whether a sense of fairness or morality evolved because it's adaptive in its own right — because it improves an individual's, and thus a species', chance for survival — then we should be able to show that more "virtuous" individuals are more fit and have more offspring than less virtuous individuals (as Darwin indicated). If play and fairness are inextricably linked (as they seem to be), then is it true that individuals who play well do better reproductively than those who don't? It's almost impossible to directly link fair play with an individual's reproductive success or fitness, but it's also extremely difficult to show with great certainty that the performance of *most* behaviors is directly and causally coupled to reproductive success. However, my students and I have collected some intriguing data on captive and wild coyotes that indicate a relationship between play and fitness.

Dogs, coyotes, and wolves are fast learners when it comes to fair play. There are serious sanctions when they breach the trust of their friends, and these penalties might indeed become public information if others see an individual cheating on his companions. Biologists call these penalties "costs," which means that an individual might suffer some decline in his or her reproductive fitness if they don't play by the expected rules of the game. Our fieldwork on coyotes has revealed one direct cost paid by animals who fail to engage in fair play or who don't play much at all. I found that coyote pups who don't play as much as others because they are avoided by others or because they themselves avoid others are less tightly bonded to other members of their group. These individuals are more likely to leave their group members and try to make it on their own. But life outside the group is much more risky than within it. In a seven-year study of coyotes living in Grand Teton National Park in Wyoming, we found that more than 55 percent of yearlings who drifted away from their social group died, whereas fewer than 20 percent of their stay-at-home peers did. Was it because of play? We're not sure, but information that we collected on captive coyotes suggested that the lack of play was a major factor in individuals spending more time alone, away from their littermates and other group members.

Though all the evidence is not in, it seems quite likely that breakdowns in social play negatively affect individuals, and by extension their social groups. In social species at least, natural selection seems to weed out cheaters, those who don't play by the accepted and negotiated rules. Conversely, animals, including humans, survive and thrive better when they play fair and learn the group's moral codes for behavior. It sure is starting to look like morality evolved because it's adaptive.

THE "BIG QUESTION": Is Morality Inherited?

They [animals] have the ingredients we use for morality.

— FRANS DE WAAL, "HONOR AMONG BEASTS"

The idea that morality may have evolved over millions of years isn't new, nor is the notion that animals share many of these behaviors. Charles Darwin proposed that human moral sentiments were a product of the evolutionary process, and he speculated about moral sentiments in animals. But it wasn't until recently that scientists gave these questions serious and sustained attention. What is emerging now is a fascinating tapestry of research into the biology of morality. We're beginning to recognize the role of morality in the lives of other species and to piece together the neurophysiological roots of moral emotion and cognition — roots that we share with other species.

Darwin's view is that morality is a natural extension and outgrowth of social instincts. Early theories of kin selection and reciprocal altruism among animals have now blossomed into a much wider inquiry into the pro-social behavioral repertoire: fairness and equity, empathy, reputation, punishment and forgiveness. At the same time, neuroscience is exploring the ethical brain: as we've seen, it is becoming clear that many moral behaviors originate in emotional centers in the brain — a neural architecture that humans share with other animals.

All of this research is confirmed by our studies of animal play. There seems to be strong evolutionary selection for playing fairly because most if not all individuals benefit from adopting this behavioral strategy, which fosters group stability. Numerous mechanisms have evolved as a result: play invitation signals, variations in the sequencing of actions performed during play when compared to other contexts, self-handicapping, and role-reversing. All these behaviors have evolved to facilitate the initiation and maintenance of social play in numerous mammals — to keep others engaged — so that agreeing to play fairly and the resulting benefits of doing so can be readily achieved. The observation from the field that play is rarely unfair or uncooperative surely indicates that natural selection acts to weed out those individuals who don't play by the rules.

This sort of egalitarianism in animals is thought to be a precondition for the evolution of social morality in humans. From where did it arise? Truth be told, we really do not know. Studies of the evolution of social morality are among the most exciting and challenging projects that we face. However, given the evidence so far, if one is a good Darwinian and believes in evolutionary continuity, it is premature to claim that *only* humans can be empathic and moral beings. At a minimum, this constitutes the safest, most cautious approach, even as research points ever more strongly toward a more "radical" notion about evolution.

ANOTHER PARADIGM SHIFT:

Survival Depends on Cooperation, Not Competition

I believe that at the most fundamental level our nature is compassionate, and that cooperation, not conflict, lies at the heart of the basic principles that govern our human existence.... By living a way of life that expresses our basic goodness, we fulfill our humanity and give our actions dignity, worth, and meaning.

— HIS HOLINESS THE DALAI LAMA, *UNDERSTANDING OUR FUNDAMENTAL NATURE*

We believe that most donkeys, if given the chance, would fashion a world without violence. Like St. Francis of Assisi, they would remake the natural world into a proverbial garden of Eden, where the lion and the lamb lay side by side.... We wonder how much the innocence, vulnerability and gentleness of [those two] donkeys may have affected Tolstoy, the peace-loving giant of world literature.

— MICHAEL TOBIAS AND JANE MORRISON, *DONKEY*

Some might call the Dalai Lama an optimist, but there are increasing scientific data to support His Holiness. Indeed, the time has come to revise our notions about what "survival of the fittest" really means.

So far, most of the research on cooperation has focused on humans. As it turns out, humans aren't as selfish and self-centered as we're sometimes made out to be. Ernst Fehr and his colleagues have discovered that when treated fairly, many people will voluntarily cooperate with one another and also punish those who don't cooperate. They call this "strong reciprocity," and they show that it can lead to "almost universal cooperation in circumstances in which purely self-interested behavior would cause a complete breakdown of cooperation." They note that people are willing to punish individuals who behave unfairly to a third person.

There's also evidence that humans have a natural tendency to be altruistic. Felix Warneken and Michael Tomasello discovered that infants as young as eighteen months of age will help people in need, such as when they're searching for a lost object. Young chimpanzees also will do this. What's very interesting about this study is that young children, while still in diapers and not very skilled in using language, will only help retrieve a lost object when they believe that a person needs the object to complete a task. For example, they would only retrieve a clothespin if it seemed to have been dropped unintentionally by the researcher, but not if it was clearly thrown on the ground deliberately. Children can understand through body language when something is needed or not, and they help only if there is a need.

Research with animals shows similar findings. Obviously, as we've seen throughout, when it comes to play, cooperation is required, and almost every piece of communication is aimed at maintaining that cooperation. But cooperation seems to predominate in a wide range of social situations. Primatologists Robert Sussman and Paul Garber report that for diurnal prosimians, such as lemurs, New World monkeys, and great apes, the vast majority of social interactions are affiliative rather than agonistic or divisive. Grooming and bouts of play predominate in the affiliative category. For the prosimians, an average of 93.2 percent of social interactions are affiliative, and the numbers for the New World monkeys and Old World monkeys are 86.1 and 84.8 percent, respectively. Unpublished data for gorillas show that 95.7 percent of their social interactions are affiliative.

Clearly, if these numbers can be repeated among other species, competition does not drive animal behavior; cooperation and friendliness aren't simply sideshows to aggression and fighting. Indeed, it almost seems trite to write about cooperation in animals, because everyone knows that animals cooperate with one another and it's obvious why they do so: if the group works together, then each individual's chance for survival improves. However, much of evolutionary theory is based on competition among individuals rather than on cooperation, and for some people this has meant that cooperation must be a by-product of competition that is not directly selected for in evolution. In this view, animals only cooperate because if they were competitive all of the time it would be difficult to form and to maintain stable social groups. For example, it would be impossible to have a stable wolf pack in which all of the males were top wolf or alpha individuals who always competed with one another. Cooperative interactions have to back competitive encounters so that the group will be cohesive and stable over time.

This "survival of the fittest" mentality, which pervades so much thinking and theorizing, is increasingly not supported by current research as being the prime mover in evolution. For a long time, cooperation has been ignored because of this ideological bias, but the recent deluge of research papers and other essays on cooperation indicate that the tide is changing. In fact, the more we look for cooperation, the more we discover its presence. Animals certainly still compete, but cooperation is central in the evolution of social behavior, and this alone makes it key for survival. When animals cooperate, they're doing what comes naturally, and cooperation relies on established, well-maintained social standards of behavior — that is, moral codes. This is what should become the starting point for evolutionary theory and the basis for our discussions about the lives of animals.

Some ecologists take this even further. They wonder if, when studying "ecological interactions" — that is, encounters among different species of animals and interactions between animals and trees and plants — it makes more sense to concentrate on positive ecological interactions rather than on competition and predation. These researchers have been called "renegade ecologists" by more mainstream scientists, and they argue that there is more to ecology and the evolution of communities than just competition and predation. They maintain that a process called "facilitation" readily works alongside competition and provides a balance to its mechanisms that is important in the evolution of community structure. However, it's one thing to say that cooperation within a group of individuals, for example a wolf pack or a troop of baboons, is beneficial — that all wolves benefit more by helping one another than by competing with one another — but is cooperation an essential component of an entire forest or ecosystem? It's an intriguing notion, one on which I'm sure His Holiness the Dalai Lama would like to see more research.

IS THERE A "UNIVERSAL" MORALITY?

Justice presumes a personal concern for others. It is first of all a sense, not a rational or social construction, and I want to argue that this sense is, in an important sense, natural.

— ROBERT SOLOMON, *A PASSION FOR JUSTICE*

It's self-serving anthropocentric speciesism to claim that we're the *only* moral beings in the animal kingdom. Social morality, as exhibited during play, is an adaptation that is shared by many animals. Behaving fairly evolved because it helped young animals acquire social (and other) skills needed as they matured into adults. Being fair is also important for maintaining well-oiled and efficient cooperative groups. There may even be cooperation between different species during group hunts. If we find consistency among different species in terms of how they cooperate and negotiate agreements to be fair, we might discover a universal morality. Such morality might also be important in acquiring, defending, and sharing food, in social grooming, and in the communal care of youngsters.

In *The Origins of Virtue*, biologist Mark Ridley points out that humans seem to be inordinately upset about unfairness. However, we don't know much about how other animals react to unfairness. Nonetheless, we are discovering some good leads to build on from observations of animals at play — and we may soon be able to include a sense of injustice as a shared trait. What about forgiveness? This is another moral sense that is often attributed solely to humans, but the renowned evolutionary biologist David Sloan Wilson shows that forgiveness is a complex biological adaptation. In his book *Darwin's Cathedral: Evolution, Religion, and the Nature of Society*, Wilson says, "Forgiveness has a biological foundation that extends throughout the animal kingdom." And further, "Forgiveness has many faces — *and needs to* — in order to function adaptively in so many different contexts. [Wilson's emphasis]" While Wilson concentrates mainly on human societies, his views can easily be extended — and responsibly so — to nonhuman animals. Indeed, Wilson points out that adaptive traits such as forgiveness might not require as much brain power as once thought. This isn't to say that animals aren't smart, but rather that forgiveness might be a trait that is basic to many animals, even if they don't have especially big and overworked brains.

It's clear that morality and virtue didn't suddenly appear in the evolutionary epic beginning with humans. The origins of virtue, egalitarianism, and morality are more ancient than our own species. While fair play in animals may be a rudimentary form of social morality, it still could be a forerunner of more complex and more sophisticated human moral systems. But perhaps most important, if we try to learn more about forgiveness, fairness, trust, and cooperation in animals, maybe we'll also learn to live more compassionately and cooperatively with one another.

CHAPTER 5

Hard Questions: Answering Skeptics and Addressing Uncertainty in Science

Sometimes I read about someone saying with great authority that animals have no intentions and no feelings, and I wonder, "Doesn't this guy have a dog?"
— FRANS DE WAAL

Ever since early childhood, I've wondered, "What is it like to be a fox?" or "What does it *feel* like to be a fox?" Through high school, college, and beyond, this interest remained, and when I discovered the field of cognitive ethology, I knew that this is what I wanted to study. My parents told me that I always "minded animals." I now understand this in two ways: I always attributed minds to animals, but I also minded them — cared for them, respected them, and loved them. This has been a central part of who I am since childhood. It's innate — my evolutionarily "old brain" pulls me back to animals and to nature. Even today I ask the same question: "What is it like to be a dog, or a wolf, or a coyote?" The difference is that today I have the training and experience to actually find out, and it is a great satisfaction to feel I've made a lot of progress in answering this question. Of course, even after almost four decades of studying animal behavior and cognitive ethology, there is still more to learn, and I'm as curious as ever.

A lot of my early animal education came from the warm and compassionate home in which I was raised. I always felt for other animals — their joy, sorrow, and pain. It was natural for me to empathize with them. I am indeed sorry for the harm that I caused animals early in my career (while doing biomedical research). I know I'm still not perfect, but I try as hard as I can to minimize harm — to be proactive, to anticipate the various stresses that different types of research might cause for animals. The course of my life changed radically — for the better — when I decided to stop causing intentional harm in the name of science. I think it's important to voice your beliefs, and so I take part in peaceful and compassionate protests on behalf of animals, from wild animals like black-tailed prairie dogs and Canadian lynx to domesticated animals in our labs and farms. On more than one occasion I've ruffled a few academic feathers by making my views known in scientific circles where they're not always accepted. Finally, I believe that scientists are responsible for sharing their findings with nonscientists. Scientists need to be less self-absorbed and more community minded.

I tell you all this because it's important to stress that science isn't value-free. Each scientist brings to his or her work a certain set of values; these influence how we conduct research and explain and interpret data. The goal of science is to reach "objective" conclusions about the world — answers that are free of personal bias — but scientists themselves are not unfeeling automatons. They're individuals, real people with particular points of view. Science has always struggled with this. At what point does subjective knowing become objective "truth"? How much research, and what kind, needs to be done to prove something? How much does a scientist's beliefs influence how he or she interprets "objective" data without being aware of this bias? Do a researcher's intuitions and feelings, the personal self, *ever* have a place in science?

These are the issues that we will address in this chapter. They are the "hard questions" that all scientists must ask of themselves and their work, but they are particularly relevant to cognitive ethology, which relies on anecdotes, analogy, and anthropomorphism to reach its conclusions. These have traditionally been "dirty words" in science, since they smack of the subjective and the personal; invariably, when scientists criticize ethology and its findings, one or all of them are mentioned. But are people who resist these three *A* words themselves reacting out of personal or professional bias? Could there be a place in science for subjectivity that doesn't compromise "objective truth"? Most pointedly of all, could the discomfort some scientists have with acknowledging animal emotions reflect, not the quality of the evidence, but fear of being seen as "unscientific"? Personally, I think that stepping out of one's comfort zone is a great educational motivator.

I love being a scientist and conducting scientific research, but I remain open to other ways of knowing, to innovative thinking. I don't think it's a matter of science *or* subjectivity but rather science *and* subjectivity. Personal truths are valid; if they are acknowledged and accounted for, they don't need to compromise objectivity. As we see below, it may very well be that emotions are not strictly personal, either, but they may have evolved as social adaptations, tools for understanding what others are feeling. In any case, we need to be able to live with uncertainty. Many scientists like the autonomy and authority society grants them, and they are loath to jeopardize their status by seeming too personal or unsure, but we must all give up control. Science and scientists must be dynamic, open, and compassionate.

Much of science is still written in the third person rather than the first person. The use of the third person — "the researcher did this" or "the subjects were observed by the researcher" — makes it easy for researchers to distance themselves from the animals they study, and even from the process of conducting their research. Third-person language allows researchers to pretend that their personal values and perspectives don't influence their results, and it reinforces the erroneous notion that science is value-free. Most important, third-person language denies not only the subjectivity of the scientist but the subjective lives of the animals being studied. Animals are subjective beings, but scientists frequently treat them like objects because that is what they are trained to do. This does a disservice to animals, to scientists, and to our knowledge of one another. If we choose to study other animals, as well as speak for them, then we should represent them with open hearts and clear minds. Our research should be both diligent and compassionate. The study of animal behavior, animal emotions, and research about the nature of human-animal interactions would surely benefit from, if not require, a more honest and open first-person approach.

BILL AND RENO:
Certain at Home, Uncertain at Work

When it comes to animal sentience and emotions, some scientists have a hard time reconciling how they act with their own pets at home with what they believe and do at work. When it comes to their pets, they treat them with the love and affection of a family member, marvel at their games and knowledge, and feel the satisfaction of being loved in return. Then they go to work, and suddenly they just can't say for sure if animals feel or know anything.

This was the case for a friend of mine, whom I'll call Bill. Before a lecture I was going to give at a major American university, Bill came up to say hello. I asked him how his dog, Reno, was doing, and for more than five minutes, Bill told Reno stories — how Reno loves to play with his friends, how he anxiously misses Bill when he's gone, and how a few days ago Reno became jealous of the attention that Bill was giving his daughter. Reno sounded like a pretty bright and emotional dog. He can be happy and sad, loves his family, and communicates all this clearly to Bill.

I was thrilled to hear these stories, as Bill has always been dubious about animal emotions. The furthest he would go was to say that animals did act "as if" they experienced an array of emotions, but it was too early to make any grandiose pronouncements about what their feelings were, or if they had them at all.

My excitement was short lived. During the question-and-answer session following my talk, Bill accused me — in a sort of light-hearted academic way — of being far too anthropomorphic and too sure of myself. I was taken aback, but instead of arguing the point, I simply asked Bill to recall for the audience the conversation that we'd had before my lecture, about Reno's emotional life. Bill turned slightly red, and then said, "Well, you know what I meant when we were talking before. I was just letting my hair down and telling stories about Reno. I really don't know that he enjoys playing with his friends or that he really is depressed when I leave him alone. And I feel rather certain that he wasn't really jealous of the attention I was giving to my daughter. He just behaved as if he were."

To be frank, I still don't really know what Bill meant. He was quite comfortable telling me about Reno's feelings in one context but not in another. Did he mean to say he lived in a fantasy world at home (in which he prefers acting "as if" animals have emotions), but returned to "reality" at work? Or did he mean that he was reluctant to behave in his job in ways, or to espouse beliefs, that were consistent with his personal experience? For whatever reason, Bill couldn't reconcile his personal and scientific selves, and he didn't even seem to recognize that there was a disconnect — or dissonance, as psychologists call it — between what he told me an hour earlier and what he said he believed at the lecture.

Similar conversations among scientists take place at cocktail parties when it's permissible to let your guard down — when scientists don't feel they need to sanitize animal emotions with all sorts of "Well, you know what I mean" disclaimers. In these settings, scientists will speak freely of their pets' intelligence and feelings, but those statements vanish once they put on the lab coat Monday morning. This distancing mechanism seems essential to allow them to conduct their work, but does it make for good science, or healthy scientists? If a scientist is conducting experiments that harm an animal they would love in another context, like a dog, wouldn't it be hard for the person to admit the animal was feeling and realizing everything he or she was doing to it? In this case, wouldn't "doubt" about animal emotions simply be a way for the scientist not to feel so bad? Or is "doubt" sometimes a fig leaf for scientists who don't want to commit the sin of bringing personal emotions to their work — and suffering the possible criticism or judgment of colleagues? I didn't have the heart to ask Bill if he would do to Reno what he does to other animals in his lab. I expect he wouldn't.

In cases like Bill's, my suspicion is that "doubt" about animal emotions is espoused not because it serves science but because it protects the emotional needs of the scientist.

ASLEEP ON THE JOB:

How Do You Know What You Know?

Bill was pretty nice about our disagreements. However, some people get more upset, and their skepticism is profound. Right after I gave a lecture on animal emotions in Bochum, Germany, a woman in the audience — who looked as bored as bored could be — stood up and accused me and other fieldworkers of always "being sleep deprived," and that's why we attribute active minds and deep feelings to animals. I tried to disarm her because I thought she was partly joking (and also because I really was sleep deprived, from jet lag!), but she became rather hostile. She was quite serious, and I wasn't sure what to say. So I answered the charge seriously: I told her that cognitive ethologists were scientists and serious researchers who didn't sleep on the job. Even if arduous fieldwork did make us tired, this wasn't the reason we wrote about animal passions. We wrote about them because we observed them in the field, and we have learned they've evolved as important adaptations. Fieldwork isn't perfect; it has benefits as well as shortcomings. Lab-bound researchers (who assign numbers to animals they study in cages) often criticize fieldworkers for being too lax and for not having control over the animals they observe. But I counter this by noting that we can gain the most complete understanding of the rich, complex lives that animals lead by observing them in their natural environments. In any case, fatigue and a lack of control can't conjure emotions out of thin air.

Similarly, I recall an event at a symposium that was held at the Smithsonian Institution in 2000. Cynthia Moss talked about her long-term research on the social behavior of wild elephants in Kenya, and showed a wonderful video of these highly intelligent and emotional beasts. During the question-and-answer period, a former program leader from the National Science Foundation asked Cynthia, "How do you know these animals are feeling the emotions you claim they are?" And Cynthia aptly replied, "How do you know they're not?" Of course, neither question could be answered with absolute certainty. Scientific research overwhelmingly supports Cynthia's view, but despite our best efforts, there remains an element of doubt.

When it comes to the interior life of any other being (including humans) — but particularly beings of another species — there may always be a point beyond which we cannot see or measure or know. The presence of some doubt doesn't call into question the whole field of cognitive ethology, however, nor does it mean that hopeful researchers are engaging in wishful thinking or spinning exhaustion-fueled fantasies. Cognitive ethologists are sincere scientists; they're trying to bring rigor to a difficult area of study, and to put forth reasonable explanations of the evidence they find. Twenty years from now, our understandings and explanations will be richer, more accurate, and possibly different; this is true in any field. When it comes to the emotional lives of animals, science is just trying to catch up to what people experience every day.

THE DALAI LAMA ISN'T WELCOME

As in any field, science has its professional prejudices, and these can hamper openness and innovation. As a rule, "hard sciences" like physics and biology are more respected than "soft sciences" that examine cognition and emotions. Genetic research and chemical processes have a concreteness, a veneer of objective certitude, that touchy-feely fields like cognitive ethology can't match. The result is that sometimes researchers in the "soft sciences" are very image conscious: they want their research to look as "serious" as possible, and their methods are indeed usually scrutinized more closely and criticized more often.

A vivid example of this occurred in October 2005. His Holiness the Dalai Lama planned to present a paper about neurotheology at the annual convention of the Society of Neuroscience, and as the date drew closer, some scientists began voicing their opinion that he should be excluded. Neurotheology is the name for the study of the neural bases of meditation and spiritual experiences. The Dalai Lama is very interested in this field of inquiry and was himself a research subject; he is a strong supporter of scientific inquiry. While the available database is small, it does suggest that there are some unique neural states — an increased level of neural activity in the left anterior temporal region of the brain — associated with meditation. Yes, more data are needed, but where isn't this the case?

Nonetheless, this particular group of neuroscientists wanted to exclude the Dalai Lama from speaking because, they argued, some of the claims about the neurobiology of meditation are unsubstantiated and not scientifically rigorous. Some also believed that "the field of neuroscience risks losing credibility if it ventures too recklessly in spiritual matters." One neuroscientist, Nancy Hayes, went so far as to opine, "If we don't [object to the Dalai Lama's presence], we may as well be the Flat Earth Society."

While the split between science and religion is overblown, it still exists in some circles, and clearly, in this case, fears over reputations and appearances led some scientists to close the door on open inquiry. When did listening to the Dalai Lama become a "reckless" act? Are the foundations of neuroscience really so shaky that they can't support research into meditation? Of course, many neuroscientists supported the Dalai Lama's visit, and world-renowned researcher Robert Wyman offered a reminder of the basis for the scientific method: "You get curious about something and you mess around. That's what science is in the beginning, you mess around." At last, the Dalai Lama was allowed in.

Though they're decreasing, the same fears and criticisms plague the field of cognitive ethology. Scientists worry that the database is too scanty to support its conclusions, and others say researchers risk their credibility for trying to study phenomena that are difficult to observe and quantify. Are critics of the Dalai Lama and of cognitive ethology afraid of what might come of this research? Would it threaten them if there were indeed ways of knowing that couldn't be captured in a test tube or placed on a slide? Critics of studies of animal minds frequently apply a double standard, demanding stronger data for research on topics such as animal consciousness and animal emotions than they require for less controversial subjects in "hard sciences" like physics, chemistry, or biomedical research.

In fact, the study of animal emotions is strongly evidence based, and in an interesting turn of events, people who do hard science are generating more and more of the data. One reason the study of animal emotions is so exciting is that the down-home observations of animals doing what they do are being supported by laboratory-bound researchers who have chosen to study the neural basis for emotions and even why humans anthropomorphize.

SPEAKING OUT:

Being Passionate about Animal Passions

Most scientists have traditionally been hesitant to speak freely about animal emotions, but times are changing rapidly. When my book *The Smile of a Dolphin: Remarkable Accounts of Animal Emotions* was published in 2000, it was a coming out party for more than fifty distinguished scientists who tell their own stories about the emotional lives of the animals they knew best, the animals with whom they had bonded during years of study. They tell stories about love in dolphins, fish, and dwarf mongooses; about anger and aggression in octopuses, ravens, and cats; of joy and grief in spotted hyenas, elephants, and rats; and of embarrassment, resentment, and jealousy in primates. These stories demonstrate that many different animals have rich emotional lives, and they also make clear that the scientists themselves have feelings for the animals they study.

Now, while this doesn't sound revolutionary to non-researchers who care about animals, for scientists to display their feelings and to write freely about animal emotions, to speak about individuals they have named rather than numbered — this was a big step forward. Events like this help legitimize the formal study of animal passions as well as legitimize the passions of ethologists. Astronomers can speak glowingly and poetically about the night sky, sharing their love for the stars, without fear that their emotions will lead anyone to doubt the reliability of their data. People understand that passion is essential; it keeps an individual going when problems arise and the hours grow long. Passion fuels the curiosity essential for scientific inquiry. And people understand that astronomers can be both passionate and meticulously accurate at the same time. To date, ethologists have not enjoyed that same presumption, though this is changing.

As it turned out, I wound up turning down the requests of a number of distinguished scientists who wanted to tell their stories about animal emotions in *The Smile of a Dolphin* because of limited space. But scientists themselves are continuing to break down barriers by discussing animal emotions in other venues and publications. No longer do researchers have to clean up their language and sanitize their prose by using quotation marks around words such as *happy*, *sad*, *jealousy*, or *grief*. No longer do they have to play verbal gymnastics about their claims. Animals don't merely act "as if" they have feelings; they have them. Scientists are free to tell their stories, and the implications of their detailed observations for how we need to treat animals are obvious to all.

ANECDOTES:

The Importance of Stories

When reviewing someone's research, scientists always consider how the data were collected, whether the data seem reliable, and how the data are finally explained, interpreted, and disseminated. Anecdotes, or stories, are a type of data, and they always find their way into people's descriptions of animals. However, some scientists dislike or ignore anecdotes because they're "merely stories." They're not "hard data" because they're not reproducible, and they're potentially too tainted with personal involvement and biases.

However, much of our theorizing about the evolution of behavior also rests, for better or worse, on stories. Few scientists find this objectionable, perhaps because these stories revolve around the widely accepted central unifying theory of natural selection. In fact, systematic analyses of anecdotes can lead to data that are reproducible by organizing experiments that mimic the anecdotal situations.

I like to say that the plural of anecdote is data. Anecdotes are central to the study of animal behavior and animal emotions, as they are to much of science, and rightfully so. Emotions don't occur in a vacuum. They occur in context; there are events that cause them, and consequences that follow, and to properly describe them means telling a story. How do we know a baboon is angry? Well, he is eating, someone takes his food, he screeches at and chases the other baboon, and then takes his food back. How do we know a young red fox misses his mother? He squeals, searches for her, and when the two are reunited, he snuggles her closely, closes his eyes, and quietly falls asleep. We could restrict our description to just the first baboon's and fox's actions and manners, but it's the theft and the mother's absence that help clarify that the screeching and chasing, or the squealing and snuggling, didn't indicate joyful play, amorous mating, or some other behavior.

As we accumulate more and more stories, we develop a solid behavior database that can be used to stimulate further empirical research, and yes, additional stories. It is important to note the frequency with which similar stories surface among different species, and that these also help us identify particular emotions. Different species may express emotions using different behaviors, but the context of the story helps make clear that the emotions are similar. Further, the more stories we gather showing the same thing, the less likely it will be that personal bias has influenced the collection of data or our conclusions. In the end, anecdotes are only data that are perhaps gathered more slowly, but that doesn't make them any less useful or reliable.

THE INEVITABLE "SIN": Anthropomorphism

It is possible, therefore, that your simple man, who lives close to nature and speaks in enduring human terms, is nearer to the truth of animal life than is your psychologist, who lives in a library and today speaks a language that is tomorrow forgotten.

— WILLIAM J. LONG, *BRIER-PATCH PHILOSOPHY BY "PETER RABBIT"*

In the late 1990s two remarkable novels were published: White as the Waves, *a retelling of* Moby Dick *from the perspective of the whale... and* The White Bone, *about the destruction of elephant society as seen by elephants.... Both novels use what is known of the biology and social lives of their subject species to build pictures of elaborate societies, cultures, and cognitive abilities. Their females are concerned with religion and environment as well as the survival of calves: their males inhabit a rich social and ecological fabric of which mating is only a small part. A reductionist might class these portraits with* Winnie-the-Pooh *as fantasies on the lives of animals. But for me they ring true, and may well come closer to the natures of*

> *these animals than the coarse numerical abstractions that come from my own scientific observations.*
>
> — HAL WHITEHEAD, *SPERM WHALES*

Along with anecdotes, anthropomorphism has frequently been used to bash the field of cognitive ethology. There are many different ways of describing what animals do. How one chooses to summarize what animals see, hear, or smell depends on the questions in which one is interested. There isn't only one correct way to describe or to explain animal behavior and emotions. In the study of animal behavior, anthropomorphism is the attribution of human characteristics to nonhuman animals. Using words that describe such human characteristics as thinking, joy, grief, embarrassment, and jealousy is to be anthropomorphic. It's a common practice that irks many of my colleagues, although most of them freely engage in it.

As the quotes that begin this section make clear, the suspicion that anthropomorphic explanations may in fact accurately describe animals has been around a long time. Perhaps William Long, writing more than a hundred years ago, could be dismissed as being "out of touch" with current research, but Hal Whitehead is recognized as one of the world's leading whale researchers, and it's clear that he sees the value of anecdotes and anthropomorphic explanations.

As humans who study other animals, we can only describe and explain their behavior using words with which we're familiar from a human-centered point of view. So when I try to figure out what's happening in a dog's head, I have to be anthropomorphic, but I try to do it from a dog-centered point of view. Just because I say a dog is happy or jealous, this doesn't mean he's happy or jealous as humans are, or for that matter as other dogs. Being anthropomorphic is a linguistic tool to make the thoughts and feelings of other animals accessible to humans. And while we surely make errors from time to time, we're pretty good about making accurate predictions in the mental realm.

If we decide against using anthropomorphic language, we might as well pack up and go home because we have no alternatives. Should we talk about animals as a bunch of hormones, neurons, and muscles absent any context for what they're doing and why? Anthropomorphism is inevitable and involuntary. Psychologist Gordon Burghardt notes that denying our own intuitions about an animal's experience is "sterile and dull." If we don't anthropomorphize, we lose important information. The renowned and influential experimental psychologist Donald Hebb, who loved to collect numbers and do statistical analyses, also made some important observations about anthropomorphism. For Hebb, zookeepers' anthropomorphic accounts proved to be "an intuitive and practical guide to behavior," enabling them to best interact with the captive chimpanzees for whom they cared. Hebb also suggested that an objective analysis of the basis of anthropomorphism might make it "suitable for the purposes of a scientific comparative psychology."

Konrad Lorenz, by studying the mechanisms that encourage human adults to nurture their young, also seems to have found part of the reason we're prompted to anthropomorphize. Lorenz noted that human beings are attracted to certain characteristics of juvenile animals, including a "relatively large head, predominance of the brain capsule, large and low-lying eyes, bulging cheek region, short and thick extremities, a springy elastic consistency, and clumsy movements." In other words, they look like human babies, and this "cute response" may be further encouraged by traits that increase the seeming "cuddliness" of an animal: fur, fuzziness, and softness of skin or hair. Anthropomorphism is clearly at work when we're drawn to young animals, and I don't know of anyone who hasn't called a puppy "cute."

In scientific circles, however, anthropomorphism is frequently a big no-no, and don't try using it with a sense of humor. Just ask Professor Robert Sapolsky, who tells the story of Nick, the pissy baboon bully, in chapter 3. "Do I get grief for the fact that in communicating, say, about the baboons I'm doing so much anthropomorphizing?" Sapolsky asks.

"One hopes that the parts that are blatantly ridiculous will be perceived as such. I've nonetheless been stunned by some of my more humorless colleagues — to see that they were not capable of recognizing that. The broader answer, though, is I'm not anthropomorphizing. Part of the challenge in understanding the behavior of a species is that they look like us for a reason. That's not projecting human values. That's primatizing the generalities that we share with them." In other words, we all recognize and agree that animals and humans share many traits, including emotions. Thus, we're not inserting something human into animals, but we're identifying commonalities and then using human language to communicate what we observe.

When we anthropomorphize, we're doing what comes naturally, and we shouldn't be punished for it. It's part of who we are. Early in her career Jane Goodall was criticized for not using scientific methods, for naming chimpanzees rather than assigning each a number, for "giving" them personalities, and for maintaining they had minds and emotions. We've come a long way since the 1960s in many areas, but unfounded fears over anthropomorphic language linger on. It's time to put them to rest, for the betterment of animals and for the betterment of science.

Among early humans, anthropomorphizing may have allowed hunters to better predict the behavior of the animals they hunted, and it's very useful for learning more about beastly passions today. Stephen Jay Gould agrees: "Yes, we are human and cannot avoid the language and knowledge of our own emotional experience when we describe a strikingly similar reaction observed in another species." Anthropomorphism endures because it is a necessity, but it also must be done carefully, consciously, empathetically, and biocentrically. We must make every attempt to maintain the animal's point of view. We must repeatedly ask, "What is that individual's experience?" Claims that anthropomorphism has no place in science or that anthropomorphic predictions and explanations are less accurate than more mechanistic or reductionistic explanations are *not* supported by any data. Careful anthropomorphism is alive and well, as it should be.

ANTHROPOMORPHIC DOUBLE-TALK:

Animals Can Be Happy, but Not Sad

When it comes to anthropomorphic language, I've noticed a curious phenomena over the years. If a scientist says that an animal is happy, no one questions it, but if a scientist says that an animal is unhappy, then charges of anthropomorphism are immediately leveled. Like the dissonant personal beliefs of scientists in the story involving my friend Bill, this "anthropomorphic double-talk" seems mostly aimed at letting humans feel better about themselves.

A good example is the story of Ruby, a forty-three-year-old African elephant living at the Los Angeles Zoo. In fall 2004 Ruby had been shipped back to the Los Angeles Zoo from the Knoxville Zoo in Tennessee because people who saw Ruby in Knoxville felt that she was lonely and sad. A videotape recorded by Gretchen Wyler, of the Humane Society of the United States, shows Ruby standing alone and swaying. Wyler said Ruby behaved like "a desperate elephant." Sad and lonely animals often rock back and forth repeatedly. This stereotyped behavior is not normal and is characteristic of bored and distressed animals.

Wyler and others who claimed that Ruby was unhappy were accused of being anthropomorphic by people who thought that Ruby was doing just fine, both in Knoxville and Los Angeles. The former director of conservation and science for the Association of Zoos and Aquariums (AZA), Michael Hutchins, claimed that it's bad science to attribute humanlike feelings to animals, saying: "Animals can't talk to us so they can't tell us how they feel." He was critical of people who claimed that Ruby wasn't doing well in captivity and was unhappy because she lived alone and had been shipped from one place to another during the past few years, leaving her friends behind.

The mayor of Los Angeles also weighed in and claimed, "She's in good spirits, and we're glad to have her back." And John Capitanio, the associate director for research at the California Primate Research Center at the University of California–Davis, made the following claim: "Do animals have emotions? Most people are willing to say they do. Do we know much more than that? Not really. . . ." Hutchins went on to discount the view that Ruby was unhappy, saying: "An animal might look agitated, but it might not be. It might be playing. It might look like it's playing, but be quite aggressive."

Hutchins is right — it's possible to mistakenly classify an animal's behavior, but it's wrong to imply we can never figure it out. Careful and detailed behavioral studies have shown time and again that we can indeed differentiate and understand animal behavior, and how it differs in various social contexts.

Does it matter whether Ruby was happy or sad? It does. If she were shown to be unhappy, the zoo would be obligated to care for her better. Zoo officials and the L.A. mayor felt very comfortable saying she was "doing well," and Hutchins and Capitanio felt it was "good science" to rebut any claims to the contrary. But seeing positive emotions in Ruby is as anthropomorphic as seeing negative emotions. In fact, anthropomorphism was not really the issue; the charge was merely a smoke screen to discredit the other side. The issue was animal welfare, and the only thing to decide — since we can't know with absolute certainty what Ruby was thinking — was whose interpretation seemed most likely, given what we do know of her history and of elephant behavior.

Hutchins and Capitanio did not specifically address elephant behavior, they addressed only their ideological "foes." But those who work with elephants know that one ignores an elephant's "mood" at one's own peril. British philosopher Mary Midgley says it well:

> Obviously the mahouts [elephant keepers] may have many beliefs about the elephants which are false because they are "anthropomorphic" — that is, they misinterpret some outlying aspects of

elephant behaviour by relying on a human pattern which is inappropriate. But if they were not doing this about the basic everyday feelings — about whether their elephant is pleased, annoyed, frightened, excited, tired, sore, suspicious or angry — they would not only be out of business, they would often simply be dead.

Inappropriate anthropomorphism is always a danger, for it is easy to get lazy and presume that the way we see and experience the world must be the only way. It is also easy to become self-serving and hope that because we want or need animals to be happy or unfeeling, they are. In fact, the only guard against the inappropriate use of anthropomorphism is knowledge, or the detailed study of the minds and emotions of animals.

MIRROR NEURONS:
Can Feelings Know?

In talking about anthropomorphism above, I've discussed it mostly as a language issue. We only have human terms to describe what we see. However, there is a deeper level. I know that I — and many other people and researchers I've talked to — feel the feelings of other animals. We feel their exuberant and boundless joy and stifling grief, their embarrassment and petty jealousy. As I watch an animal, I'm not reaching for the closest word to describe the behavior I see; I'm feeling the emotion directly, without words or even a full, conscious understanding of the animal's actions.

Is this just the effect of my living in Boulder, Colorado, at an elevation of six thousand feet? Perhaps, but a series of recent studies seem to support my impression that I can feel what animals are feeling and that I'm not projecting my own, unrelated emotions. My feelings actually know what's going on inside the animal, and this emotional empathy seems to be innate.

The most intriguing studies about shared feelings involve "mirror neurons." This is the name given to a part of the brain that seems to allow us to understand another individual's behavior by imagining ourselves performing the same behavior and then mentally projecting ourselves into the other individual's shoes. To what degree various species share this capability remains to be seen, but there is compelling evidence that it exists, and humans are not alone in possessing it.

Research by Vittorio Gallese, Giacomo Rizzolatti, and their colleagues at the University of Parma in Italy, suggests a neurobiological basis for sharing intentions, which they discovered in their studies of macaque monkeys. In 2006, Dr. Rizzolatti was quoted in the *New York Times* as saying: "It took us several years to believe what we were seeing. The monkey brain contains a special class of cells, called mirror neurons, that fire when the animal sees or hears an action and when the animal carries out the same action on its own." He went on to say, "Mirror neurons allow us to grasp the minds of others not through conceptual reasoning but through direct simulation. By feeling, not by thinking." Researchers believe that mirror neurons might also be used in other modalities such as hearing and smelling.

Research on mirror neurons is truly exciting, and the results of these efforts will be very helpful for answering questions about which species of animals may have "theories of mind" or "cognitive empathy" about the mental and emotional states of others. Gallese and philosopher Alvin Goldman suggest that mirror neurons might "enable an organism to detect certain mental states of observed conspecifics...as part of, or a precursor to, a more general mind-reading ability." Laurie Carr and her colleagues discovered, by using neuroimaging in humans, similar patterns of neural activation both when an individual observed a facial expression depicting an emotion and when he or she imitated the facial expression. This research suggests a neurobiological underpinning of empathy. And British researchers Chris and Uta Frith have also reported results of neural imaging studies in humans that suggest a neural basis for one form of "social intelligence," or the means by which we understand others' mental states.

More data are needed to determine if mirror neurons, or neurons that work like them, are found in other species, and if they might actually play a role in the sharing of intentions or feelings — perhaps as keys to empathy — between individuals. Evolutionary continuity points to the reasonable conclusion that it's highly likely they do exist in many different species. Again, there might be mirror neurons for sensory modalities other than vision. Many animals communicate their feelings using sounds and odors as well as visible behavior.

Any of the stories of empathy in chapter 1 are good examples of behavior most likely driven by mirror neurons. Here is another one: Hal Markowitz's research on captive Diana monkeys shows them engaging in behavior that strongly suggests empathy. Individuals were trained to insert a token into a slot to obtain food. The oldest female in the group failed to learn how to do this. Her mate watched her failed attempts, and on three occasions he approached her, picked up the tokens she had dropped, inserted them into the machine, and then allowed her to have the food. The male apparently evaluated the situation, only helped his mate after she failed, and seemed to understand that she wanted food but could not get it on her own. He could have eaten the food, but he let his mate have it. There was no evidence that the male's behavior benefited him in any way other than to help his mate. Similarly, scientists at the Max Planck Institute for Evolutionary Anthropology, in Leipzig, Germany, discovered that captive chimpanzees would help others get food. When a chimpanzee sees that his neighbor can't reach food, he will open the neighbor's cage so the monkey can get to it. Mirror neurons also help explain observations of rhesus monkeys who won't accept food if another monkey suffers when they do so, and of empathic mice who react more strongly to painful stimuli after they observed other mice in pain.

Finally, evidence is surfacing that anthropomorphism may be a hardwired mode for conceptualizing the world in general, not just other animals. Recent research by Andrea Heberlein and Ralph Adolphs shows that the brain's amygdala is used when we impart intention and emotions to inanimate objects or events, such as when we talk about "angry" weather patterns or "battling" waves. Heberlein and Adolphs studied a patient called SM who had damage to the amygdala and discovered that SM described a film of animated shapes in entirely asocial and geometric terms, though the patient had normal visual perception. Their research suggests that the "human capacity for anthropomorphizing draws on some of the same neural systems as do basic emotional responses." My reading of this research and my own experience with animals is that "We feel, therefore we anthropomorphize." And we're programmed to see humanlike intentions and mental states in events where they cannot possibly be involved.

Anthropomorphism is a much more complex phenomenon than we would have expected. It may very well be that the seemingly natural human urge to impart emotions to animals — far from obscuring the "true" nature of animals — may actually reflect a very accurate way of knowing. And the knowledge that is gained, supported by much solid scientific research, is essential for making ethical decisions on behalf of animals.

CHAPTER 6

Ethical Choices: What We Do with What We Know

Ethics in our Western world has hitherto been largely limited to the relations of man to man. But that is a limited ethics. We need a boundless ethics, which will include the animals also.... The time is coming when people will be amazed that the human race existed so long before it recognized that thoughtless injury to life is incompatible with real ethics. Ethics in its unqualified form extends responsibility to everything that has life.

— ALBERT SCHWEITZER,
MEMOIRS OF CHILDHOOD AND YOUTH

Clearly, we know a lot about animal emotions. While we obviously have much more to learn, what we *already know* should be enough to inspire changes in the way we treat other animals. We need to turn our knowledge into action. We must not simply continue with the status quo because that is what we've always done. What we know has changed, and so should our relationships with animals. We must reflect on the fact that many animals experience passion and suffering — they feel love and pain — and then consider all the ways we currently treat animals in our society and decide what is right and what is wrong. When we recognize something that is wrong, we should work to change it.

Animals are companions with whom we share our homes. They are our food. They are on display in our zoos, and they fill our scientific research labs. They also live "freely" in the wild, on the edges of a human civilization that constantly encroaches on them. We need to look at all these areas (and more) and decide if we are caring for animals properly. Frequently, we are not, and as a society there are many reasons we should be ashamed of how we interact with other animals. We need more checks and balances in our interactions. We disregard and silence sentience routinely.

Sentience is the central reason to better care for animals. Questions regarding sentience are important and extremely challenging, but we also need to distinguish between feeling and knowing. *Well-being centers on what animals feel, not what they know.* Does it really matter if monkeys in a zoo, rats in a lab, or cows on a farm ever understand what is going on around them, or what is being done to them by humans, if they can feel pain and experience suffering? Animals in these situations depend on us completely, and their behavior tells us when they're healthy and happy, or in pain and sad. Animals can't call 911 in an emergency; they depend on our goodwill and mercy. While animals can't consent to how they're being treated, they surely protest publicly when they're suffering. Their pain is easy to see and is all too often ignored.

When I give talks, some people become defensive and point out all the ways that humans *do* care for animals. And it's true; many people go to great lengths to treat, nurture, and rescue animals, and there are some wonderful stories to tell about this. However, I stress that very often what passes for "good welfare" in our society simply isn't good enough. Humans often make distinctions between how they treat "smart" animals and "dumb" animals, and particularly in institutional settings, animal care usually deteriorates significantly as it becomes less convenient (i.e., less profitable or an impediment to "progress"). This isn't good enough. We must provide the best welfare to *all* animals *all* of the time and work toward not using them at all.

Our thinking regarding animals and science has changed a great deal in the last century. It was only a hundred years ago that writers and naturalists who gave animals "personalities" were vilified as "nature fakers," a movement that was initiated by John Burroughs and strongly supported by Teddy Roosevelt. Their targets were naturalists such as Ernst Thomas Seton, William J. Long, and Jack London. Science was supposed to be objective and value-free, and mixing "facts" with ethics, values, and emotions was taboo, so "sham naturalists" like London and others were charged with sentimentalizing science. Their nature writing was considered fictional.

That was then. Now we know better. We know that "objective, value-free science" itself reflects a particular set of values. We know that the results of scientific research (all those facts) *should* influence how we act in the world; otherwise, science becomes a meaningless exercise. And we also know animals feel emotions and suffer at our hands, and they do so globally. Ethics, with a capital *E*, needs to have a place in our ongoing deliberations about how we interact with other animals. And I mean ethics the way Socrates did, as the notion of "how we ought to live." Ethics requires a critical appraisal of who we are and what we do, as well as a vision of what we want to be. Ethics helps us evaluate the best course of action when there are several options and our information is incomplete, conditional, or conflicting. We may never reach our ideal vision, but it's necessary to formulate one so that we have guidance to make the best choices.

When it comes to our relationships with animals, our vision of who they are and what they mean to us requires that we change the way we have always treated them. We know that animal beings are not "things" that exist for our convenience. Animals are subjective beings who have feelings and thoughts, and they deserve respect and consideration. We don't have the right to subdue or dominate them for our selfish gain —

to make our lives better by making animals' lives worse. Further, as self-conscious, sentient beings ourselves, we are able to recognize suffering, and we are obliged to reduce it whenever we can. By making decisions that help animals, we add compassion, not cruelty, to a "wounded world," as the ecologist Paul Ehrlich calls it.

There is much that we can do, and much that is relatively easy to do. This chapter looks at a few of those positive things, while providing a quick appraisal of the current state of affairs for animals in the lab, on the farm, at the zoo, and in the wild. But first I have a few more things to say about doubt and action.

THE PRECAUTIONARY PRINCIPLE

> *The nature of science is that it never (well, hardly ever) yields answers that are complete and unequivocal, but the consensus among scientists is that most, if not all the animals that we use for our own purposes, whether for food, for fun or for scientific procedures, are sentient. The simplest definition of animal sentience is "Feelings that matter."*
>
> — JOHN WEBSTER,
> *ANIMAL SENTIENCE AND ANIMAL WELFARE*

> *Because uncertainty never disappears, decisions about the future, big and small, must always be made in the absence of certainty. Waiting until uncertainty is eliminated is an implicit endorsement of the status quo, and often an excuse for maintaining it.... Uncertainty, far from being a barrier to progress, is actually a strong stimulus for, and an important ingredient of, creativity.*
>
> — HENRY POLLACK,
> *UNCERTAIN SCIENCE... UNCERTAIN WORLD*

Henry Pollack was speaking about attitudes toward climate change, but his remarks apply equally well to the study of animal emotions and animal sentience. Pollack was describing what many scientists call the precautionary principle, which guides the actions of people around the world every day, though they are not always aware of using it. Basically, this principle maintains that a lack of certainty should not be an excuse to delay taking action. Sometimes we have to act based on our best judgment, because we may never have "all" the facts, and if we wait for absolute certainly, we might never do anything.

With respect to animal emotions, I believe we know as much as we need to, and more than we think we do, to change, right now, the way we treat animals. We may never know everything that goes through an animal's mind and heart, but we don't need to. As a society, we just need to ask ourselves, What would cause more harm? What has higher consequences? Treating mammals, birds, fish, and reptiles as if they possessed the full spectrum of emotions and sentience only to one day discover that animals possess only *some* of these qualities? Or continuing to abuse all animals only to one day discover that *every* species possesses sentience and an emotional richness equal to humans? Guinea pigs and elephants would surely appreciate our use of the precautionary principle.

However, for some people, acknowledging that animals possess emotions is unnerving because of how society currently treats them. What we don't know, or supposedly don't know, makes it easier to avoid feeling guilt or remorse over the inhumane treatment many animals are subjected to. This is true for the scientists I talk about in chapter 5, and it is also true for average folks, zoo administrators, and food company employees. But when the basis for one's doubts is eroded, one is left with only denial — by not acknowledging the rich emotional lives of animals, we can avoid invoking the precautionary principle and changing how we treat them.

Ideally, most people, scientists included, would act only when they're sure. We love to be in control. But certainty is difficult to find in this complex world. We don't really know much about the causes of the common cold or whether or not living near power lines causes health problems, but we try not to take unnecessary risks. As a society, we are unnecessarily risking the lives and welfare of millions of animals every day. We do this, in part, because animals are integral to so many essential aspects of our lives, from the food on our tables to the medicines that heal us, and we see no other way. Solutions that account for animal emotions seem too complex to envision, and they seem like they would entail too many sacrifices on our part. But we need to do something besides deny the problem. As Henry Pollack encourages us, our doubts and concerns should become the fuel for our creativity. Surely, there must be ways we can care for animals and meet society's needs at the same time. Even if we can't always achieve a perfect balance, we should certainly explore every possible option we can think of. Animals deserve at least that much consideration, and our ethics should demand it.

IN THE LAB:
Take a Number

As a scientist myself, I tend to get the most upset about animal abuse in the lab. It's probably unrealistic and self-centered, but I think that scientists should hold themselves to higher standards than nonscientists. I feel this way not just because the actions of one thoughtless scientist reflect badly on all scientists, but also because the rest of society often takes their cues from us. If scientists, who should know better, feel free to treat animals like disposable objects, then that gives permission to others to do the same. However, were scientists to insist on only conducting humane research because it was the right thing to do, then it might be much harder for others to justify animal abuse.

How many animals are used in labs? By one count, in 2001 American laboratories conducted research on about 690,800 guinea pigs, rabbits, and hamsters, in addition to 161,700 farm animals, 70,000 dogs, 49,400 primates, 22,800 cats, and 80 million mice and rats. These numbers are small compared to the billions of animals used in commercial food industry, but this is still a lot of animals. The vast majority of these animals live most of their lives in extremely small cages, bored and lonely, and they will die in the lab when researchers are done with them: almost all are killed by researchers — either deliberately, because dissecting them is part of the research and sacrificing them outright clears the way for naive new subjects, or as an unintended consequence, because the animals just couldn't cope with what was being done to them.

The scientific community has created a set of professional standards that is supposed to guide scientists to preserve animal welfare as much as possible in their research. In theory animals used in research in the United States are protected by the Animal Welfare Act. But so far it has proven inadequate. Only about 1 percent of animals used in research in the United States are protected by this legislation, and the legislation is sometimes amended in nonsensical ways to accommodate the "needs" of researchers. For instance, here is a quote from the 2004 federal register: "We are amending the Animal Welfare Act (AWA) regulations to reflect an amendment to the Act's definition of the term animal. The Farm Security and Rural Investment Act of 2002 amended the definition of *animal* to specifically exclude birds, rats of the genus *Rattus*, and mice of the genus *Mus*, bred for use in research."

It may surprise some people to hear that birds, rats, and mice are no longer considered animals. Since researchers are not "allowed" to abuse animals, the definition of "animal" is simply revised until it refers only to creatures whom researchers use less frequently, even if they are sentient and empathetic beings.

Horror Stories: From the Lab to the Island of Dr. Moreau

Tales of extreme abuse grow increasingly rare, and I truly believe that many scientists sincerely try to do their best for the animals in their care. But even "everyday" stories of lab work can sometimes make me feel sick and woefully sad. For instance, the Animal Welfare Act legally allows chimpanzees to be kept in cages as small as five feet square and seven feet high. This legislation certainly aids labs by saving space, but where is the welfare for the chimps? In response to the recent discovery that mice are empathic rodents, it was suggested that an opaque barrier be used to separate mice so that they can't know what's happening to another mouse. This is because mice who observe each other during experiments may change their behavior as a consequence and therefore "contaminate" the data. I'm sure if you saw what was going on in the other cage, you'd prefer not to see it either.

Even scientists who see what's going on can sometimes have trouble breaking through the veneer of their own jargon-garbled "objectivity" and telling it like it is. To read their convoluted explanations is to feel like you've entered the theater of the absurd. Recently, I read a report about pain in pigs that concluded:

> The observed changes of acoustical parameters during the surgical period can be interpreted as vocal indicators for experienced pain and suffering. We conclude that a careful analysis of the vocal behavior of animals may help to gain a deeper knowledge of pain, stress and discomfort that an animal perceives. The results deliver further facts for a critical re-evaluation of the current practice of non-anaesthetized castration of piglets.

What this is saying is that castrating young pigs without anesthesia, a routine procedure in domestic pig production, is painful. The piglets don't like it, as evidenced by their squeals and attempts to get out of their horrible situation. The researchers conclude that it can be "interpreted" — a far cry from concluding the obvious — that the screams of animals really mean something after all.

Some scientists willingly push the legal boundaries of what's permissible, no matter how much pain and suffering they cause. For instance, using a $500,000 taxpayer-funded grant provided by the U.S. Department of Justice, a University of Wisconsin professor attached electrodes directly to the skins of pigs and implanted catheters near their hearts to measure the effects of Taser shocks. In this way, live pigs were electrocuted to death in order to satisfy claims that Tasers are safe. Then there were psychologist Harry Harlow's well-known maternal deprivation studies in monkeys, in which the good doctor decided to study the nature of mother-infant bonds by taking infant monkeys away from their mothers to see what would happen. Is there any question in anyone's mind what happened? More to the point, are the questions these researchers are seeking to answer so desperately vital that they justify suffering, and even death?

I believe there are times when trading new knowledge for fewer traumas is a worthwhile exchange. But what's especially disturbing is that often the knowledge gained in animal research isn't even used to make human or animal lives better — because the people who are in the position to implement the new findings are unaware they even exist. Psychologist Kenneth Shapiro, in his book *Animal Models of Human Psychology*, shows this to be true in the case of animal models of human eating disorders.

As well, species differences often preclude the utility of animal models for helping humans, a point well made by, among others, physician Ray Greek and his veterinarian wife, Jean. In February 2006 the prestigious Diabetes Research Institute published a report stating that "scientists from the Diabetes Research Institute at the University of Miami Miller School of Medicine have shown that the composition of a human islet is so different than that of the rodent model, it is no longer relevant for human studies." And, in an essay published in the *Journal of the American Medical Association*, it's been estimated that 106,000 people die each year in hospitals from adverse reactions to drugs that had previously been tested on animals and were approved by the Food and Drug Administration. Adverse drug reactions is the fifth leading cause of death in the United States following heart disease, cancer, stroke, and lung disease.

Finally, there are scientists who, if they think they can get away with it, ignore any legal and ethical boundaries to conduct their work. For years, there were unsubstantiated allegations that the Oregon Regional Primate Research Center (ORPRC) was violating federal animal welfare laws. In 1998 Matt Rossell took a job there to find out. During the course of his undercover investigation, he documented a number of outrageous cruelties, such as the basic living conditions: at the time, about a thousand monkeys lived in the laboratory, many of them in tiny and often filthy cages not much larger than four feet square. But by far the most horrific practice Rossell observed was "electro-ejaculation." This involved strapping an unanesthetized adult male monkey into a restraining chair, wrapping two metal bands around the base of his penis, and applying an electrical charge to cause ejaculation. The procedure was performed in order to collect semen samples. The monkey, number 14609, was nicknamed "Jaws" because one of his supervisors taught him to bite the bars of his cage. Until the procedure was banned as a result of Rossell's investigation, Jaws underwent electro-ejaculation on 241 separate occasions from 1991 to 2000, not counting the times when his penis was shocked more than once during a session to get the semen needed. No wonder Jaws tried so desperately to escape the ordeal. In the end, a veterinarian resigned and some of the scientists working there made critical statements about conditions in the laboratory, but ORPRC continues to operate.

Professional Standards: The Three Rs

Among scientists, it's commonly accepted that there aren't any substitutes for animal research, and that it's necessary for the development of vaccines and medicines, as well as an aid to understanding biological and cognitive processes, and of course for the development of commercial products, from dyes to Tasers, to make sure they don't harm humans. Yes, some researchers think they should be able to do whatever they want to the animals with whom they work, but the great majority tries to minimize the suffering their research causes. Of course, many procedures that seem like "necessities" today merely demonstrate a lack of creativity; as we'll see, when researchers really emphasize animal welfare, they're finding noninvasive ways to get the information they need.

In any case, the long-standing professional guidelines that most scientists follow are called "the Three Rs": this refers to *refining* procedures that cause harm to animals, *reducing* the number of animals used, and *replacing* animals with other methods whenever possible. The term "the Three Rs" was proposed by William Russell and Rex Birch in their 1959 book *The Principles of Humane Experimental Technique*. The Three Rs call attention to the fact that animal welfare is important. Practicing scientists are not supposed to merely give lip service to this. They are expected to do all they can to minimize the impact of research on animals, or to eliminate such research if they can.

The Three Rs are guidelines, however, not laws or an official code of conduct. No one reviews a scientist's planned research and suggests alternatives. Each individual decides how religiously to follow the Three Rs, and in practice, the Three Rs are often sacrificed in the name of expediency. In the rush to find a treatment or a cure for this or that disease, it's easy for scientists to justify more animal research, using invasive techniques they are familiar with (and that often kill the animal), rather than think up more humane alternatives. And they do this despite the fact that animal testing provides no guarantees — huge numbers of people continue to suffer or die even after drugs or other treatments have been tested "successfully" on animals. In practice, the false hope of animal research is an enormous waste of money and life.

In fact, there is a plethora of data that shows that animals who are treated humanely and who are not stressed produce "better data." This doesn't justify animal research, but it does call attention to the fact that if animals aren't properly cared for, much of the information that is collected is compromised and even useless. If scientists actually upheld the Three Rs, not just when it was convenient but at all times, it would make for better science, better data, and a more compassionate world.

Some say life is too short to ponder if animals have feelings, and I agree. However, I also feel that life is too *long* to ponder whether animals have emotions. The suffering that numerous animals endure while some researchers try to figure out if they're feeling anything at all is unacceptable and cruel.

Bad Data: The Effects of Cages and Isolation

Much of the research on animals is conducted in captivity where animals are often stressed. Stressed animals don't behave like unstressed individuals, and particularly when it comes to animal emotions and behavior, information that's collected on anxious or bored animals doesn't have much to say about the normal behavior of individuals of the same species. Scientist Françoise Wemelsfelder notes that the term "boredom" is often used to interpret the abnormal behavior of animals who are permanently housed in small barren cages.

Wemelsfelder defines boredom as "the impaired ability to actively focus attention upon, and interact with, the environment." Bored animals spend more time sitting, lying down, and sleeping than do more stimulated individuals, and bored animals may also overreact to novel or unexpected events with increased fear and aggression. They also perform repetitive, stereotyped behavior, such as pacing back and forth or bar biting. To quote Wemelsfelder:

> Sometimes such behavior can be damaging to other animals; licking and nibbling tails and ears of offspring may for example induce cannibalism in rats and mice. As time of confinement proceeds, such patterns tend to become increasingly directed towards the animal's own body or products thereof. Primates may spend long periods of time masturbating, rocking their own body, or eating and regurgitating their own feces. Rats may chase their own tail, tethered sows may show long bouts of chewing air, with no other apparent effect than producing large amounts of saliva. Such tendencies may eventually develop into various forms of compulsive

self-mutilation. Laboratory monkeys gnaw at their own limbs or genitals, while parrots will pull out their feathers until completely naked. In summary, the overall decrease in interaction shown by captive animals comes to expression in a decrease in behavioral variability and an increase in self-directed behaviors.

These behavior patterns may sound "abnormal," but they're actually "normal" responses to being kept in barren cages with few if any social companions or objects. Wemelsfelder notes, "They bear a strong resemblance to behavior pathologies in human beings. It is generally accepted that in human beings, abnormal behavior may be a sign of depression, or other forms of subjective suffering." Thus, one unintended result of most lab work is to further demonstrate that animals have emotions and can experience suffering. In a series of excellent research papers on abnormal repetitive behaviors (ARBs), Georgia Mason and her colleagues have shown that at least ten thousand captive wild animals in zoos worldwide show these stereotypes. As a result of this groundbreaking research, Mason et al. call for "zero tolerance of such ARBs" because they indicate poor individual welfare and clearly raise serious ethical issues.

Wemelsfelder has studied boredom in animals in great detail and has discovered that boredom can be alleviated using environmental enrichment, which consists of providing toys, straw, bedding, and social companions. Making animals work for their food also has been useful for reducing boredom. Rabbits and other animals react to more stimulating environments by showing increased activity and breeding success, and decreased aggression.

"If such measures are combined to enhance the active, flexible character of species-specific behavior," Wemelsfelder argues, "both the well-being of captive animals and the quality of scientific research benefits significantly." In other words, happy animals make for better data. They become a more "normal" model for scientific investigation, and their responses to experimental situations is more, rather than less, stable and consistent. In one Dutch scientific laboratory, environmental enrichment led to a considerable decrease in the number of animals needed for experimentation — precisely because happier animals enhanced the reliability of the experiment's results. This clearly shows caring for the well-being of animals and seeking to understand their needs and requirements can go hand in hand with enhancing the quality of scientific research. It's also known that enriching the lives of captive animals makes for happier caretakers; it increases the well-being of the people responsible for the care of the animals.

It's also been shown that the richness of a primate's environment affects the animal's brain structure and learning abilities. Professor Charles Gross conducted a study of marmosets that suggests that bored monkeys make for stupid monkeys. In the study, pairs of adult marmosets were housed in one of three types of cages for one month. The first was a bare cage with a food bowl, which actually meets the minimum standards of the National Institutes of Health (NIH). The second was a slightly larger cage with toys and structures, including branches hiding live worms, that encourage the monkeys to forage. The third cage was twice as big with many more toys.

Unfortunately, the marmosets used in this study were killed so that their brains could be examined. Gross learned that the animals housed in the second two cages developed denser neuron growth and almost double the amount of certain synaptic proteins that the brain uses to relay messages between neurons. He suggests that it may be necessary to house animals being used for cognitive studies in more stimulating environments than those specified by the NIH. Indeed. Even further, now that this particular study has been conducted, whether or not it should have been, there is no reason to repeat it and kill the monkeys we are trying to learn how to care for better.

Noninvasive Research: Better Science through Technology

Traditionally, animal research involving cognition, behavior, and emotion ends with the death of the animal so that the brain can be cut up, blended, or otherwise analyzed. But it seems strange to me that scientists would consider it normal to kill a mind to study a mind. Thankfully, a growing number of scientists agree that it's strange, and they are developing a number of noninvasive research techniques that improve and preserve the lives of the animals being studied, and this, as we've just seen, also improves the quality and reliability of the information collected.

In one study done on living dolphins, Dorian Houser and his colleagues investigated how hearing and echolocation are processed in dolphin brains. By using brain scans, they monitored blood flow in what's called the melon of the dolphin brain, the part that's responsible for processing information about the clicks used in communication. Houser even took pains to reduce anxiety by giving the dolphins diazepam when their brains were scanned.

Research that stresses and harms animals often produces misleading data, which makes it difficult to find answers to the very questions in which we're interested. But we can learn a lot from looking at brains at work by using methods that minimally stress the animals or humans being studied. What has been particularly exciting and important in this regard is the use of noninvasive neural imaging techniques, such as functional Magnetic Resonance Imaging (fMRI) and positron emission tomography, also known as PET scans. These imaging techniques give researchers the ability to localize the activity of the brain when people, and in some cases animals, are in a specific social situation. As with the studies of mirror neurons, fMRI and PET scans are providing solid neurobiological proof for much of what we suspected all along when it comes to cognition and emotions, confirming, for example, the huge hippocampus in elephants. The field of social neuroscience is rapidly growing and will produce a lot of interesting information in the coming years about empathy, forgiveness, cooperation, mother-infant interactions, and emotions in general.

So far, fMRIs have been used mainly on people, not animals. However, they have been used successfully on squirming baby humans, so it's possible that in the not-too-distant future, other animals — many of whom tend not to hold still either — might be studied using this noninvasive and informative technique. When this is accomplished, it should be possible to study cognitive processes and emotions in awake animals.

Here's just one exciting example of how powerful these methods of study really are when it comes to animal research. James Rilling and his colleagues have used PET scans to study the neural response to staged social interactions in dominant male rhesus monkeys. The researchers set up a situation in which nine dominant males were faced with a "challenge situation," in which they witnessed a potential sexual interaction between a rival male and their mate, and a control situation in which only their female consort was present with no potential rival. In preparation for the PET scan, the monkeys were injected with a fluorescent dye and then sedated so that their blood could be drawn and measurements of the brain's uptake of the dye could be assessed; however, the monkeys didn't have to be killed, as usually happens in studies like this. Researchers were especially interested in male sexual jealousy — they fearlessly used the *J* word — when males are challenged in having exclusive access to their mates. They discovered similarities between how sexual jealousy is expressed in humans and in these monkeys, and they found there might also be a similar neural network involved in the expression of vigilance or wariness and anxiety shown by a challenged male.

I can only hope that more examples of humane research will lead to better treatment of animals everywhere. One of my favorite bumper stickers reads: "Back off man, I'm a scientist!" This is funny because it's true: many researchers arrogantly believe they should never be questioned, about their methods or their goals. But let's not back off. We should always ask hard questions and make sure science and scientists are held accountable for their treatment of animals.

ON THE FARM:
The Meat We Eat

While numerous animals are used for research, education, clothing, amusement, and entertainment, their numbers pale when compared to the numbers of animals used for food. And while the treatment of animals in these other settings can often range from thoughtless to reprehensible, it doesn't compare to the horrific ways in which food animals are treated. In recent years, several good exposés of factory farming and the meatpacking industry have been published, so I will not spend much time cataloging agriculture's sins. However, if ever there were an area where our society should begin practicing the precautionary principle in regards to animal sentience, this is it. If we are what we eat, then what we eat sometimes redefines cruelty.

The numbers are astonishing. In 1998 in the United States alone, more than 26.8 billion animals were killed for food — that translates to about 73,424,657 animals per day, 3,059,361 animals per hour, 50,989 animals per minute, and 850 animals per second. It's hard to conceptualize that much death occurring in a single afternoon, and then there's the appalling squalor of today's factory farms. The worst slums in the human world do not compare to the ways many cows, chickens, and pigs spend their entire lives: crowded into tiny cages and small fenced lots; standing, eating, and sleeping in mud and their own feces; and having their lives ended by a mechanical butcher. In fact, as many as 12 percent of chickens and 14 percent of pigs die of stress, injury, or disease before they are mature enough for the slaughterhouse.

Not that these weakened animals are "wasted." Many times they find themselves in containers called "4-D bins," which stands for the Dead, Dying, Diseased, and Disabled. Animals in 4-D bins are used in commercial pet food; they are the ones eaten by our companion animals.

Thankfully, people are noticing. The movement toward raising "free-range" chickens and livestock is one way farms can mitigate the worst abuses. Governments are occasionally stepping in too: by 2012, the European Union has pledged to phase out wire battery cages, which are the crowded 67-inch-square prisons into which chickens are stuffed. These cages are too small to allow chickens to stand upright, and they are unable to stretch, unfold their wings, or exercise. What's more, they suffer various injuries. Considering the scale of the problem, these are minor efforts, but they are at least pointed us in the right direction. Additionally, in October 2006 Germany banned seal products.

The Vegetarian Solution

> *As we talked of freedom and justice one day for all, we sat down to steaks. I am eating misery, I thought, as I took the first bite. And spit it out.*
> — ALICE WALKER, "AM I BLUE?"

I decided to become a vegetarian solely for ethical reasons. I didn't want to be part of the chain of inhumane treatment that slaughters sentience and characterizes the factory farming of beings from cows to pigs to chickens to fish to lobsters. One of my colleagues says that the main question that motivates people in the industry is, "How many chickens can you get in a cage with Vaseline and a shoehorn?" One day, I figured that I should start practicing what I preach. I realized I could no longer abide the killing of any animal, no matter how humane the process, simply for it to become my meal. It was actually an easy decision, and it hasn't changed my lifestyle or my cycling one bit. In fact, it immediately made me feel better.

Many people are deeply conflicted about the food they eat. What we eat, how it's grown, how it's processed, where it comes from, who profits, who's exploited: there are a wide range of complex issues to consider, and individuals must decide for themselves what is the most healthy for their own body and soul. Some people consider themselves vegetarians, although they aren't strict: they may still eat fish, or perhaps occasionally eat other meat (such as for a holiday meal), or restrict themselves to "animals without faces." For example, some people are willing to eat animals such as faceless scallops or mussels because they believe they're not sentient and do not suffer. This may or may not be true, but it's where some people drawn the line for themselves. Rather than vegetarians, these people are what Peter Singer and Jim Mason call "conscientious omnivores" in their book *The Way We Eat*.

Ethical issues aside, there are other reasons to consider opting out of the meat economy. One major one is environmental. The feedlots and slaughterhouses of factory farms are responsible for enormous environmental degradation. According to Lucas Reijinders and Sam Soret, compared to soy production, meat production takes more land (6 to 17 times as much), water (4.4 to 26 times), fossil fuels (6 to 20 times), and biocides (6 times as many pesticides and chemicals used in processing). Though it sounds funny, cows are also a significant source of methane. To quote James Bartholomew: "A single dairy cow belches and farts 114 kilos of methane a year. It is a methane machine. Methane is far more lethal as a greenhouse gas... than carbon dioxide. It is 23 times more potent, although it does not last so long in the atmosphere. The methane produced by a single cow is equivalent to 2,622 kilos of carbon dioxide." Furthermore, according to Philip Fradkin, the feeding of livestock is still the single greatest use of the dwindling amount of water in the western United States.

While I realize that, despite my wishes, ours isn't going to become a vegetarian world anytime soon, if ever, I also don't understand why arguing for one is considered "radical." Is it radical to recognize that animals have emotions and to allow them their passions? I believe a vegetarian world would be a more compassionate world. However, no matter what we decide to do or call ourselves, so long as we are "conscientious," so long as we carefully scrutinize how we choose our meals — so long as we eat mindfully, as Jane Goodall puts it — then surely we can reduce the intentional harm that we cause to billions of sentient animals.

IN THE ZOO:

Cages, Conservation, and Entertainment

People are entertained by exotic animals at zoos, but is this reason enough to put animals through the tribulations of being trapped and taken from their natural environments, separated from their families, housed in cages, and put on public display seven days a week, including holidays? No, which is why zoos operate with two express purposes: one is to educate the public about animals and conservation, and the other is to help preserve species.

These are laudable goals, but they rest on two shaky premises. One is that zoos can actually succeed at them, and the other is that zoos can adequately care for their charges. As for their goals, there is insufficient evidence to know the extent to which zoos actually educate visitors or if zoos play any significant role in species protection. Even the Association of Zoos and Aquariums (AZA), which oversees U.S. zoos and grants accreditation if they meet certain standards, acknowledges in its *own* executive summary that "Little to no systematic research has been conducted on the impact of visits to zoos and aquariums on visitor conservation knowledge, awareness, affect, or behavior." Meanwhile, AZA's conservation and management program, called the Species Survival Plan (SSP), attempts to ensure the survival of certain wildlife species using managed breeding programs, conducting basic and applied research, training wildlife and zoo professionals, and reintroducing captive bred wildlife to their proper habitat. These things certainly sound good, but there is widespread skepticism about their application. Terry Maple, director of Zoo Atlanta, has been quoted as saying, "Any zoo that sits around and tells you that the strength of zoos is the SSP is blowing smoke."

So if zoos don't really educate and aren't important for species survival, can they at least be trusted to nurture their animals? Unfortunately, too often the answer is no.

Bad Report Card: Flunking the National Zoo

Zoos exist in the real world; they have budgets, good and bad managers, and limitations. Zoos are not perfect. But what does it say when one of the nation's largest and most high-profile zoos — the National Zoo in Washington, D.C., which is run by the Smithsonian Institution — can't do a proper job of caring for its residents?

In 2005 the National Research Board on Agriculture and Natural Resources released the results of an investigation into the National Zoo. The purpose of the inquiry was to "identify strengths, weaknesses, needs and gaps in the current infrastructure." The investigation was initiated because of suspicions of mismanagement and inadequate animal treatment; in particular, public alarms had been raised when two red pandas died after being exposed to rat poison, and the safety managers, who could have prevented these unnecessary deaths, were nowhere to be found. The National Research Board asked a number of knowledgeable people to read and comment on the resultant report, and I was one of them.

In short, the report showed that large numbers of animals had suffered from their time in the National Zoo. There was a long history of major problems, and numerous infractions of federal statutes, laws, and other guidelines, not to mention a lack of plain common sense. Altogether, the violations the report cataloged were inexcusable and went beyond anyone's expectations. I was sickened by what I learned.

I had several major concerns. These included the lack of documentation for the preventative medicine program and the lack of compliance in providing annual exams, vaccinations, tuberculosis tests, and infectious disease testing. Despite the zoo's supposed world-class research, there were shortcomings in the animal nutrition program that, to quote the report, had "undoubtedly lead to animal deaths at the National Zoo." In terms of research, there was disregard for guidelines supported by the Public Health Service, the Animal Welfare Act, AZA itself, and Institutional Animal Care and Use Committees (IACUCs), in addition to disregard for the zoo's own policies and procedures for animal health and welfare. The zoo did not adhere to guidelines for euthanasia, it violated quarantine procedures and protocols, and it had poor pest control. It also displayed poor record keeping in a number of areas and failed to provide adequate accessibility to the records it had.

One of the most egregious violations was the alteration of veterinary records. This was particularly disquieting because infractions and abuses occurred even though the zoo's veterinarians are board-certified by the American Veterinary Medical Association. While it was obvious that many people who work at the National Zoo care deeply about the resident animals, there was a shameful lack of concern for animal welfare by some administrators responsible for overseeing the zoo's operation.

What did AZA do in light of this report? The association has the power, after all, to withhold accreditation from zoos that don't meet acceptable standards. But even with deplorable and inexcusable conditions and the continued lack of a strategic plan for the zoo — and this last "despite the recommendations of previous AZA accreditation reports" — AZA renewed the National Zoo's accreditation in March 2004. This was done even though the review committee concluded there was "a lack of evidence that the administration has embraced its role in providing for animal care and management, compounded by a lack of responsibility and accountability at all levels." These are strong words. The report was supposed to foster significant changes, but many problems were blatantly ignored. It's hard not to conclude that the problems at the National Zoo are problems that extend into AZA as well.

There is one last bizarre twist to the National Zoo story. When Ryma, a much-loved giraffe, died at the zoo, the zoo's director said she couldn't release information about why she died because that "would violate the animal's right to privacy and would be an intrusion into the zookeeper-animal relationship." Taking this reasoning seriously (rather than as a blatant attempt to hide information that was damaging to the zoo), I have to ask a series of questions. Courts of law don't recognize animals' right to privacy, but if they have such a right, why does the zoo place them on public display without their consent for all to see, as they eat, bathe, court, mate, and sleep? It seems ridiculous to claim confidentiality as in a human patient-doctor relationship, for how would Ryma's reputation have been compromised, and with who, if her medical records were released? Would the other giraffes have been embarrassed if they knew other humans knew? But finally, and most important, if animals have the right to privacy, why don't they have the right to be free?

Too often we're intentionally misled about zoo conditions and the welfare of the animals who are dependent on our care, and there is as yet not enough information to know what effect zoos have on people's attitudes toward and knowledge of animals. This question has been little studied even by AZA's own admission. We must demand more, for far too many animals suffer every day in zoos.

The Elephant in the Room: Suffering in Plain Sight

In the past few years a number of elephants have died in captivity. The death of an elephant is a significant event for any zoo, and it is always noticed by the public. In June 2006 an elephant named Gita died in the Los Angeles Zoo, and *Time* magazine immediately responded with an essay entitled "Are Zoos Killing Elephants?" It's a fair question. Elephants are emotional, very social, and like to roam, and by definition, zoos are antithetical to these needs.

For instance, in spring 2001 Asian elephants were regularly moved in and out of the Denver Zoo as if they were couches being moved from room to room. The Rocky Mountain Animal Defense and I got involved because of the lack of concern demonstrated by both AZA and the Denver

Zoo. To wit, Dolly, a thirty-two-year-old female, was removed from her friends, Mimi, forty-two, and Candy, forty-nine, and sent to Missouri on her "honeymoon," as the zoo called it, to breed. A few months later, Hope, a mature female, and Amigo, a two-and-one-half-year-old male (who had been taken from his mother), came to the Denver Zoo, where they lived next door to Mimi and Candy. In the following months, Mimi got increasingly agitated; in June 2001 she pushed Candy over, and Candy had to be euthanized. Two days after Candy died, and a day after she was autopsied within smelling distance of the other elephants, Hope escaped from her keepers and rampaged through the zoo. Luckily, no one was seriously injured. Hope was then transferred out of the zoo, and a new elephant, Rosie, was brought in.

Elephants live in matriarchal groups in which social relationships are enduring and deep. Their memory is legendary. Elephants form lifelong relationships and grieve when bonds are broken because of separation or death. When elephants move in and out of groups, there can be severe disruption of the social order and individuals can get very upset. This is what happened at the Denver Zoo. Mimi reacted to Dolly's leaving, and Hope reacted to Candy's death and autopsy. Were these happy elephants? Absolutely not. The way they were treated is standard operating procedure for zoos, and it led to suffering and death.

And what about Maggie, an African elephant who lives alone at the Alaska Zoo in Fairbanks? She walks about aimlessly, often in snow, and gets no exercise or social companionship. It's obvious even to zoo officials that she needs help, but their answer was to spend more than $100,000 to build a treadmill for Maggie that she didn't even use! Tex Edwards, director of the Alaska Zoo, has said, "I think we're trying to do the right thing." But there is nothing "right" about keeping an elephant in these conditions; doing so ignores the wealth of information that we have about the social and emotional lives of elephants. Why not send Maggie south to a sanctuary so that she can live in a more suitable climate, with friends? That is the humane and "right" thing to do.

Broken Families, Lost Friends

What is true for elephants is equally true for most other animals. Zoos can't simply tend to an animal's physical needs and call it a day. Animals also have social and emotional needs, and just as in humans, disrupting or ignoring them leads to negative consequences. Animals have families and friends, and they know when they are missing.

I witnessed this myself when over the course of eight years, I and my students studied coyotes living in Grand Teton National Park in Wyoming. One female we called "Mom," since she was mother and wife, began leaving her family for short forays. She'd take off and disappear for a few hours and then return to the pack as if nothing had happened. We wondered if her family missed her when she left, so we observed what happened. Eventually, Mom's forays lasted longer and longer, often a day or two, and before she'd leave, some pack members would look at her curiously — they'd cock their heads to the side and squint and furrow their brows, as if to ask, "Where are you going now?" Some of her children would even follow her for a while. Then when Mom returned, they would greet her effusively by whining loudly, licking her muzzle, wagging their tails like windmills, and rolling over in front of her in glee. Clearly, her kids and mate missed Mom when she was gone.

One day Mom left the pack and never returned. The pack waited impatiently for days and days. Some coyotes paced nervously, expectantly, and others went off on short trips only to return empty-handed. They would travel in the direction she'd gone, sniff in places she might have visited, and howl as if calling for her. For more than a week, some spark seemed to be gone. Her family missed her. We believe the coyotes would have cried if they could. Their behavior told a story of deep and complicated feelings.

After a while, life returned to usual, almost. A new and unfamiliar female joined the pack, formed a partnership with the dominant male, and gave birth to ten coyote pups over two years. She became mother and wife. But every now and again it seemed that some of the pack members still missed their mom. The coyotes would sit up, look around, raise their noses to the wind, go off to look for her on short trips in the direction in which Mom had disappeared, and return weary and alone.

It was three or four months before these searches ended. Perhaps, despite their feelings, enough was enough. The life of the pack had to continue on. For coyotes in the wild, this recovery and healing from loss is possible. For coyotes held in the artificial confines of a zoo, it is infinitely more difficult. Zoos ship animals from one zoo to another for economic reasons, or simply to redecorate their exhibits in order to keep the public interested, but the vast majority of animals form close social and familial bonds, and all that moving around can have a devastating impact on an individual's well-being.

Emotional Enrichment: Tending to the Heart

As I've said, many, even most, zoo employees care deeply about the animals in their care; most often, animals suffer because their needs don't match the needs of the zoo business, not because their everyday human caretakers are cruel. And in fact, there are always folks who recognize the emotional needs of these sometimes desperate animals and find ways to soothe and help them.

Though it isn't a zoo, the International Exotic Feline Sanctuary in Boyd, Texas, is an interesting example. Here, Louis Dorfman and Scott Coleman use what they call "emotional enrichment" to better the lives of the captive exotic cats for whom they've become responsible. Dorfman and Coleman take in cats who cannot be released into the wild. With patience and careful attention to individual needs, the sanctuary works to reduce each cat's stress and rebuild a trusting and affectionate relationship with humans, who will be their caretakers. The emotional enrichment is in the form of plain human contact, which doesn't have to be direct or physical. This simple gesture of acknowledgment, attention, and caring is enough to reassure the animal and foster change, and it works for cats of different personalities and various emotional needs.

Then there is a zoo in the Netherlands that is thoughtfully tending to the emotional needs of captive orangutans in Indonesia, where these apes are kept in small cages because loggers have destroyed their homes. Webcams and monitors have been set up in both places so that orangutans in Indonesia can meet other orangutans in the Netherlands. And it seems to be working based on the gestures and facial expressions that the orangutans direct toward the screens. Also, the webcam films will provide a record of the orangutan's behavior for future reference.

Finally, I'll close with an elephant story. Recently, Suma, a forty-five-year-old elephant in the Zagreb Zoo in Croatia, was extremely upset after her partner, Patna, died of cancer. Soon after, Suma's keepers discovered that she took comfort in Mozart's music — for she relaxed and "leaned against the fence, closed her eyes and listened without moving the entire concert." The music helped Suma cope with her grief, and zoo authorities bought a stereo and provided music therapy for her.

While Suma's life is more enriched, I hope she will soon be moved to a place where she can enjoy the company of other elephants. Indeed, I hope that it's not too long before all elephants are moved from zoos to more hospitable sanctuaries. Some zoos agree. In 2006 the *New York Times* reported that "The Bronx Zoo...had announced that upon the death of the zoo's three current elephant inhabitants, Patty, Maxine and Happy, it would phase out its elephant exhibit on social-behavioral grounds — an acknowledgment of a new awareness of the elephant's very particular sensibility and needs." Zoos in Detroit, Chicago, San Francisco, and Philadelphia are following suit.

Zoos likely are here to stay in the short term, but I favor phasing them out and moving their residents to more favorable environs. The Association of Zoos and Aquariums should also enforce higher standards for accreditation and reaccreditation. Money saved could go toward protecting animals in their natural habitats, preserving critical habitat, and humane education. But, while zoos remain, we must satisfy the physical and emotional needs of all their residents — they are the reasons zoos exist, and it is our obligation to provide them with the best lives possible.

IN THE WILD:

Civilization and Its Discontents

We are part of a generation of shame, where future generations will look back on our treatment of animals and be appalled.

— JILL ROBINSON, FOUNDER OF ANIMALS ASIA

Domesticated humans have a long and troubled history with the wilderness that exists at the edges of their civilization. We try to tame it and keep it at bay, but we almost never just leave it alone. Perhaps we can't, and it's not really our fault. Wilderness is considered "wild" for a reason: it grows where it likes and has its own rules, and it rarely respects the artificial lines — the fences and park borders — we draw to contain it.

Though wild animals would seem to fall outside the responsibility of humans, we in fact need to care for them too — precisely because we already try to "manage" the wilderness for our own benefit. As our cities and suburbs continue expanding, as we claim more and more acreage for grazing and farmland, wilderness shrinks, and this habitat loss can be deadly. Animals who are accustomed to ranging for hundreds of miles struggle with these limitations, and it forces them to encroach on our human civilization. When they do, we don't like it: deer ruin our gardens and predators kill our sheep, and so we kill them to protect what we've built. In most of the American West, native predators, such as grizzly bears and wolves, have been eradicated. It's a vicious cycle. One way to ease or mitigate this would be to pay more attention to how and where we build and live. As much as possible we need to account for the natural habitats and habits of wild animals to ease these conflicts, which are inconvenient and expensive to us and deadly for them. A workable strategy would be to preserve wildlife corridors such as those proposed by the Yellowstone to Yukon (Y2Y) conservation initiative. Y2Y proposes a system of corridors that would enable grizzlies and other animals to move freely in this mountain ecosystem.

Numerous wild animals are killed by federal agencies. In 2004 the U.S. Fish and Wildlife Service killed more than 2.7 million animals. This included almost 83,000 mammalian carnivores — such as wolves, coyotes, mountain lions, and other large predators. They did so using traps, leg and neck snares, and poison. Also, they shot animals from aircraft and pulled them out of dens. And they did all of this despite mounting evidence that such killing usually doesn't solve whatever problem they've identified.

For instance, in Colorado, deer and elk suffer from chronic wasting disease, and in 2001 the state worried that continued spread of the disease would harm its hunting industry. Therefore, the Colorado Division of Wildlife began a program of deer and elk killing with the intention that — follow the logic here — more animals would survive so hunters could kill them. However, by 2006 local newspapers reported that "Officials acknowledge that killing deer and elk to contain the spread of chronic wasting disease hasn't worked." Unfortunately, they reached this conclusion only after 2,300 animals had been killed by the program.

Using the same logic, others argue that wolves are predators who kill too many elk, so the wolves should be killed to ensure that hunters have enough animals to shoot at. If anything, prey animals belong to their predators along with whom they've coevolved; wild animals aren't "our animals" to pursue and kill. But studies have shown that wolves don't significantly decrease populations of elk, deer, and other ungulates. Furthermore, wolves typically kill weak and sick individuals, whereas hunters often seek out trophy animals who are breeding stock for future generations. Wolves have also been killed to protect livestock, but short of killing every single wolf (which nearly happened by the end of the nineteenth century), this effort is also ineffective. Jim Pissot, executive director of

Defenders of Wildlife Canada, says his group has found that wolf culls don't work, and his organization is trying to raise money to help ranchers cover the costs of protecting livestock. In a separate detailed and comprehensive study, conservation biologist Kim Murray Berger has also shown that government-subsidized predator control that involves killing coyotes doesn't result in preventing a decline in the sheep industry.

Whatever short-term benefits killing wild animals provides, these don't work for the long term. Killing is easy, but it's not a lasting solution. Wild animals abide by their evolutionary behaviors, and then they adapt to the encroachments of our civilization, and it is only by our definitions that they become "pests" or "nuisances." It is incumbent on us to curb ourselves, our expectations, and our "boundaries" to reduce conflicts with wild animals. Peaceful coexistence is possible without having it depend on eliminating the other side.

US AND THEM, OR JUST US?

If we continue to allow human interests to always trump the interests of other animals, we will never solve the numerous and complex problems we face. We need to learn as much as we can about the lives of wild animals. Our ethical obligations also require us to learn about the ways in which we influence animals' lives when we study them in the wild and in captivity, and what effects captivity has on them. As we learn more about how we influence other animals, we will be able to adopt proactive, rather than reactive, strategies.

The fragility of the natural order requires that people work harmoniously so as not to destroy nature's wholeness, goodness, and generosity. The separation of "us" (humans) from "them" (other animals) engenders a false dichotomy. This results in a distancing that erodes, rather than enriches, the numerous possible relationships that can develop among all animal life. What befalls animals befalls us. A close relationship with nature is critical to our own well-being and spiritual growth.

And independent of our own needs, we owe it to animals to show the utmost unwavering respect and concern for their well-being.

Recently, I came across the word *solastalgia*, which was coined by British professor Glenn Albrecht. It describes "the distress caused by the lived experience of the transformation of one's home and sense of belonging and is experienced through the feeling of desolation about its change." We experience solastalgia when we erode our relationships with other beings.

It's easy to become anthropocentric and forget that humans are fellow animals. Our species is different, but it's also the same. Theologian Stephen Scharper resolves this contradiction with his idea of an "anthroharmonic" approach to the study of human-animal interrelationships. This view "acknowledges the importance of the human and makes the human fundamental but not focal." We are all in the world together. We and other animals are consummate companions, and we complete one another. Theologian Thomas Berry expresses this same idea a little differently. He says each and every individual is part of a "communion of subjects," in which our shared passions and sentience provide the foundation for a closely connected community. No one is an object or an other; we are all just us.

When we're unsure about how we influence the lives of other animals, we should give them the benefit of the doubt and err on the side of the animals. It's better to be safe than sorry. Many animals suffer in silence, and we don't even realize this until we look into their eyes. Then we know. In 1979 the British Farm Animal Welfare Council created the "Five Freedoms of Animal Welfare," and these have since been adopted by developed nations as the basis for their treatment of animals: freedom from hunger and thirst, freedom from discomfort, freedom to express normal behavior, freedom from fear and distress, and freedom from pain, injury, and disease. We should strive to provide these freedoms in every context in which we interact with other animals. In fact, they describe conditions that all animals, humans included, should be allowed to enjoy.

PERSONAL CHOICES, PERSONAL RESPONSIBILITY

First they ignore you, then they ridicule you, then they fight you, and then you win. — GANDHI

What do we do with what we know? When it comes down to it, we each must make our own decisions, our own choices, and take responsibility for our own actions. Individual responsibility is critical. The problems that animals face, and that we face in caring for them, can be overwhelming. It's easy to become discouraged, it's easy to feel lost and powerless, and it's easy to put the blame on institutions and corporations, on "society," and fail to address our own behavior.

How do I decide what to do? Simply put, I try to make kind choices; I try to increase compassion and reduce cruelty. I'm certainly far from perfect, but these goals motivate me daily. They guide me when I'm not sure what's right. When I challenge people, usually scientists, by asking, "Would you do it to your dog?" I'm really just trying to remind them to act with compassion. I'm trying to shock them into remembering the Golden Rule: Do unto others as you would have them do unto you.

In practice, this means walking through the world treating every living being like an equal — not the same, but as a being with an equal right to life. The Golden Rule applies to human animals, other animals, trees, plants, and even earth itself. My colleague Jessica Pierce says that we need more "ruth," a feeling of tender compassion for the suffering of others. Ruth is the opposite of ruthless, being cruel and lacking mercy. I agree. Kindness and compassion must always be first and foremost in our interactions with animals and every other being in this world. We need to remember that giving is a wonderful way of receiving.

Living up to this simple pledge is not easy. Believe me, I know. To do so, we must overcome fear — fear of going against the grain, fear of coming out of the closet, fear of ridicule, fear of losing grant money or irritating colleagues, and fear of admitting what we've done or are doing to other sentient animals. Sometimes, when we find it difficult to overcome our fears, a debilitating feeling of shame can paralyze us, but we must remember that every day brings new opportunities. No matter how small the gesture, any time we act with compassion and do what we feel is right, despite the negative consequences (whether actual or imagined), we make a difference, and that difference matters.

In March 2006 I gave a lecture at the annual meetings of the Institutional Animal Care and Use Committees in Boston. I was received warmly and the discussion that followed my lecture was friendly, even though some in the audience were a bit skeptical of my unflinching stance that we know that certain animals feel pain and a wide spectrum of emotions. After my talk, a man came up to me who's responsible for enforcing the Animal Welfare Act at a major university. He admitted that he'd been ambivalent about some of the research that's permitted under the act, and after hearing my lecture, he was even more uncertain. He told me that he'd be stricter with enforcing the current legal standards, and he would work for more stringent regulations. I could tell from his eyes that he meant what he said, and that he understood that the researchers under his watch would be less than enthusiastic about his decision. But he needed someone to confirm his intuition that research animals were suffering, that the Animal Welfare Act was not protecting them. I was touched and thanked him. Then he put his head down, mumbled, "Thank you," and walked off.

I'm an optimist and really believe that with hard work, diligence, and courage we can right many of the wrongs that animals suffer at our hands. There are many wonderful people working in a myriad of ways, large and small, to make the lives of animals better. Some efforts are very public, and some are private, but together they help to realize a peaceable kingdom here on earth, in which all beings are blanketed in a seamless tapestry of compassion and love. Surely, no one can argue that a world with more respect, compassion, and love would not be a better place in which to live and to raise all of our children. My message is a forward-looking one of hope. We must follow our dreams.

All I ask is that you reflect on how you can make the world a better place; chiefly, how you can contribute to making the lives of animals better. Do this when you're alone, away from others, so that you can feel free to look deeply and assess your current habits and actions absent peer or any other sort of pressure. It's always a sobering experience to try to view ourselves as we really are. In this case, ask yourself, how do my current actions affect other animals, and what can I do differently to care for animals better? Even when a situation is beyond my ability to change it, I make a point of apologizing to each and every individual animal who finds himself or herself being unintentionally or intentionally subjected to inhumane treatment. I believe that even just the expression of compassion can make a positive difference in the life of someone who is suffering. Silence is the enemy of social change.

We owe it to all individual animals to make every attempt to come to a greater understanding and appreciation for who they are in their world and in ours. We must make kind and humane choices. There's nothing to fear and much to gain by being open to deep and reciprocal interactions with other animals. Animals have in fact taught me a great deal: about responsibility, compassion, caring, forgiveness, and the value of deep friendship and love. Animals generously share their hearts with us, and I want to do the same. Animals respond to us because we are feeling and passionate beings, and we embrace them for the same reason.

Emotions are the gifts of our ancestors. We have them and so do other animals. We must never forget this.

Endnotes

This section contains information about the sources I used in writing this book. I've also included websites for summaries of many of the technical papers. Many of the sources for which I've included websites can be found in the archives of Ethologists for the Ethical Treatment of Animals (EETA), at www.ethologicalethics.org.

Foreword

For more information about the Jane Goodall Institute, please visit www.janegoodall.org.

Chapter 1

1 *what we see outside tells us lots about what's happening inside:* Patricia McConnell also makes this point in her book *For the Love of a Dog: Understanding Emotion in You and Your Friend* (New York: Ballantine Books, 2006).

3 *a group of fourteen elephants crashed through a village:* Reuters, "Indians Flee as Elephants Search for Dead Friend," Planet Ark, October 11, 2006, http://www.planetark.com/dailynewsstory.cfm/newsid/38452/story.html.

6 *Charles Darwin, the first scientist to study animal emotions systematically:* The complete works of Darwin, along with details about Darwin's work on emotions, can be found at http://darwin-online.org.uk/.

6 *"While I feel confident that elephants...":* Joyce Poole, "An Exploration of a Commonality Between Ourselves and Elephants," *Etica & Animali* (September 1998): 85–110.

9 *"The owner says without special intonation...":* Konrad Lorenz, *Man Meets Dog* (New York: Routledge, 1954/2002).

10 *as Alexandra Horowitz and I have argued:* Alexandra C. Horowitz and Marc Bekoff, "Naturalizing Anthropomorphism: Behavioral Prompts to Our Humanizing of Animals," *Anthrozöos* (2007).

10 *animals are frequently used to develop:* J. P. Webster, P. H. L. Lamberton, C. A. Donnelly, and E. F. Torrey, "Parasites as Causative Agents of Human Affective Disorders? The Impact of Anti-psychotic, Mood-stabilizer and Anti-parasite Medication on *Toxoplasma gondii*'s Ability to Alter Host Behaviour," *Proceedings of the Royal Society of London, Series B: Biological Sciences* 273 (2006): 1023–1030; and "Antipsychotic Drug Lessens Sick Rats' Suicidal Tendencies," *New Scientist* 2536 (January 28, 2006), http://www.newscientist.com/channel/health/mg18925365.000.html.

11 *a similar story about two grizzly bear cubs:* Doug O'Harra, "Russian River Orphans Stick Together," *Anchorage Daily News*, September 23, 2005, http://www.adn.com/news/alaska/story/7002282p6903756c.html.

11 *a story of a troop of about a hundred rhesus monkeys:* "The Depths of Feeling," *BBC Wildlife*, July 2002, http://ww.bbc.co.uk/nature/animals/features/246index.shtml.

11 *a hungry rhesus monkey would not take food:* S. Wechlin, J. H. Masserman, and W. Terris Jr., "Shock to a Conspecific as an Aversive Stimulus," *Psychonomic Science* 1 (1964): 17–18.

11 *a more recent scientific study on empathy in mice:* D. J. Langford et

al., "Social Modulation of Pain as Evidence for Empathy in Mice," *Science* 312 (2006): 1967–1970; and Ishani Ganguli, "Mice Show Evidence of Empathy," *The Scientist*, June 30, 2006, http://www.thescientist.com/news/display/23764/#23829.

12 *I received numerous stories about empathy:* I received these stories partly because I run the website for the organization Ethologists for the Ethical Treatment of Animals, which Jane Goodall and I cofounded. For more about this organization, please visit www.ethologicalethics.org.

13 *"The reluctance of contemporary philosophers..."*: Dale Jamieson, "Science, Knowledge, and Animal Minds," *Proceedings of the Aristotelian Society* 98 (1998): 79–102.

13 *A few animals have been shown to display self-awareness, such as chimpanzees, dolphins, and elephants:* Elephants only recently joined chimpanzees and dolphins, in the eyes of human researchers, as "self-aware" animals. See Andrew Bridges, "Mirror Test Implies Elephants Self-Aware," Associated Press, October 31, 2006; and Joshua Plotnick, Frans de Waal, and Diana Reiss, "Self-recognition in an Asian Elephant," *Proceedings of the National Academy of Sciences* 45 (November 7, 2006).

14 *One common measuring stick is called "relative brain size"*: More information about relative brain size can be found at http://serendip.brynmawr.edu/bb/kinser/Int3.html.

14 *"The human animal is the only animal that thinks about the future..."*: Daniel Gilbert, *Stumbling on Happiness* (New York: Alfred A. Knopf, 2006): 4.

14 *the capacity for empathy sets the human brain apart:* Gerald Hüther, *The Compassionate Brain: How Empathy Creates Intelligence* (Boston: Trumpeter, 2006): 114.

16 *a visit from a friendly pup might be good medicine:* Ed Sussman, "AHA: Cardio, the Canine Heart Dog, Is a Friend Indeed," *MedPage Today*, November 17, 2005, http://www.medpagetoday.com/Psychiatry/AnxietyStress/tb/2166.

16 *three lions in Ethiopia rescued a twelve-year-old girl:* Anthony Mitchell, "Three Lions Save Girl, 12, from Kidnap Gang," *The Scotsman*, June 22, 2005, http://news.scotsman.com/international.cfm?id=684912005.

17 *a pod of dolphins circled protectively around a group of swimmers:* Reuters, "Dolphins Protect Swimmers from Sharks," *MSNBC*, November 23, 2004, http://www.msnbc.msn.com/id/6565810/?GT1=5809.

17 *a lioness adopted a baby oryx:* Saba Douglas-Hamilton, "Heart of a Lioness," January 2002, http://www.douglas-hamilton.com/films/lioness/index.htm.

17 *a rat snake named Aochan befriended a dwarf hamster:* Associated Press, "Hamster, Snake Best Friends at Tokyo Zoo," MSNBC, January 24, 2006, http://www.msnbc.msn.com/id/10903211/.

17 *Mary and Dan Heath claim that their adult golden retriever, Chino:* JoNel Aleccia, "Friendship at the Water's Edge," *Ottaway Mail Tribune*, May 2001, http://www.mailtribune.com/archive/2001/may/053101n2.htm.

19 *Shared emotions and their gluelike power:* There is even a field of study, called anthrozoology, devoted to human and nonhuman animal interactions. For more information, check out the website for the International Society for Anthrozoology (ISAZ), at www.vetmed.ucdavis.edu/CCAB/isaz.htm.

19 *are responsible for this country's billion-dollar pet industry:* Information on pets in U.S. households comes from the following websites: www.appma.org/press_industrytrends.asp and www.hsus.org/pets/issues_affecting_our_pets/pet_overpopulation_and_ownership_statistics/us_pet_ownership_statistics.html.

19 *Jane Goodall's Roots & Shoots program:* For more information on Roots & Shoots, visit the website at www.rootsandshoots.org.

21 *"More than any other species, we are the beneficiaries…":*

R. J. Dolan, "Emotion, Cognition, and Behavior," *Science* 298 (2002): 1191–1194.

25 *Jasper is a moon bear who was formerly kept in a crush cage:* Jill Robinson told the author Jasper's story via personal email, which is the source of the quotes.

25 *animals are "a neutral palette on which we paint our needs":* P. W. Biederman, "Soft Under Her Thick Skin?" *Los Angeles Times*, November 16, 2004; this article can be found in the archives at www.ethologicalethics.org.

27 *Pablo was a captive and mistreated chimpanzee:* the source for Pablo's story is J. D'Agnese, "An Embarrassment of Chimpanzees," *Discover* (May 2002): 42–49.

Chapter 2

29 *"What we believe* Equus asinus *most prefers...":* Michael Tobias and Jane Morrison, *Donkey: The Mystique of Equus asinus* (Tulsa, OK: Council Oak Books, 2006).

31 *rats often take a moment to reflect on what they've learned:* Nicholas Wade, "Rats in a Maze Take a Moment to Remember, But in Reverse," *New York Times*, February 14, 2006, http://www.nytimes.com/2006/02/14/science/14rats.html?ex=1297573200&en=dda62d91599ce98a&ei=5088&partner=rssnyt&emc=rss.

32 *"I formerly possessed a large dog...":* Charles Darwin, *The Expression of the Emotions in Man and Animals*, third edition (New York: Oxford University Press, 1872/1998): 58.

33 *"There is no fundamental difference between man and the higher animals...":* Charles Darwin, *The Descent of Man and Selection in Relation to Sex* (New York: Random House, 1871/1936): 66.

34 *Tinbergen, Konrad Lorenz, and Karl von Frisch won the Nobel Prize:* For more information about these ethologists (and others), see the following books: Richard W. Burkhardt Jr., *Patterns of Behavior: Konrad Lorenz, Niko Tinbergen, and the Founding of Ethology* (Chicago: University of Chicago Press, 2005); Hans Kruuk, *Niko's*

Nature: The Life of Niko Tinbergen and His Science of Animal Behavior (New York: Oxford University Press, 2004); and I. Eibl-Eibesfeldt, *Ethology* (New York: Holt, Rinehart, & Winston, 1975).

37 *reptiles, such as iguanas, maximize sensory pleasure:* Michel Cabanac, "Emotion and Phylogeny," *Journal of Consciousness Studies* 6 (1999): 176–190.

Chapter 3

43 *"Much of chimpanzees' nonverbal communication is similar . . .":* Jane Goodall and Ray Greek, "The Sad Lot of Lab Chimps," *Boston Globe*, February 17, 2006, http://www.boston.com/globe/editorial_opinion/oped/articles/2006/02/17/the_sad_lot_of_lab_chimps/.

44 *Research by Sam Gosling and his colleagues has shown*: For more on Gosling's research, consult the following: Sam Gosling, "From Mice to Men: What Can We Learn about Personality from Animal Research?" *Psychological Bulletin* 127 (2001): 45–86; Sam Gosling and O. P. John, "Personality Dimensions in Non-human Animals: A Cross-species Review," *Current Directions in Psychological Science* 8 (1999): 69–75; Sam Gosling, P. J. Rentfrow, and W. B. Swann Jr., "A Very Brief Measure of the Big Five Personality Domains," *Journal of Research in Personality* 37 (2003): 504–528; and Sam Gosling and S. Vazire, "Are We Barking Up the Right Tree? Evaluating a Comparative Approach to Personality," *Journal of Research in Personality* 36 (2002): 607–614.

46 *Extensive research by Françoise Wemelsfelder and her colleagues:* For more on Wemelsfelder's research, consult the following: Françoise Wemelsfelder, E. A. Hunter, M. T. Mendl, and A. B. Lawrence, "The Spontaneous Qualitative Assessment of Behavioural Expressions in Pigs: First Explorations of a Novel Methodology for Integrative Animal Welfare Measurement," *Applied Animal Behaviour Science* 67 (2000): 193–215; Françoise

Wemelsfelder and A. B. Lawrence, "Qualitative Assessment of Animal Behaviour as an On-farm Welfare-monitoring Tool," *Acta Agriculturae Scandinavica* 30 (2001): 21–25 (supplement); and Françoise Wemelsfelder and M. Farish, "Qualitative Categories for the Interpretation of Sheep Welfare: A Review," *Animal Welfare* 13 (2004): 261–268.

46 *"The question is whether people agree in the judgments . . . ":* Françoise Wemelsfelder, E. A. Hunter, M. T. Mendl, and A. B. Lawrence, "Assessing the 'Whole Animal': A Free-Choice-Profiling Approach," *Animal Behaviour* 62 (2001): 209–220.

47 *Other researchers have come to the same conclusion:* In the following study, naive observers were found to be very good at distinguishing between friendly, playful interactions and fighting in wolves: R. E. Anderson, J. Ryon, and J. C. Fentress, "Human Perception of Friendly and Agonistic Wolf Interactions," *Aggressive Behavior* 17 (1991): 58.

47 *"He is a hot-blooded, 30-year-old male . . . ":* "The Word: Musth," *New Scientist*, February 11, 2006, http://www.newscientist.com/channel/sex/mg18925381.900.html;jsessionid=OEMHPOFBBJLN.

48 *it was declared that Leonardo da Vinci's* Mona Lisa *was actually happy:* "Mona Lisa 'Happy', Computer Finds," *BBC News*, December 15, 2005, http://news.bbc.co.uk/1/hi/entertainment/4530650.stm; and Associated Press, "Was Mona Lisa Pregnant When She Posed?" MSNBC, September 27, 2006, http://www.msnbc.msn.com/id/15029288/.

49 *"The elephants came at all times of the year . . . ":* M. J. Owens and D. Owens, *Secrets of the Savanna* (Boston: Houghton Mifflin, 2006): 2.

49 *"But most disturbing of all, in Blue's large brown eyes . . . ":* Alice Walker, "Am I Blue?" in *Living by the Word* (New York: Harcourt Brace Jovanovich, 1988): 8.

49 *"The last time I looked into Five's eyes . . . ":* Doug Smith, "Meet

Five, Nine, and Fourteen, Yellowstone's Heroine Wolves," *Wildlife Conservation* (February 2005): 33.

50 *"It was those eyes more than anything...":* Charles Siebert, "The Animal Self," *New York Times Magazine*, January 22, 2006, http://www.nytimes.com/2006/01/22/magazine/22animal.html?ex=1161662400&en=0e4659dbbfad212e&ei=5070.

50 *the well-known story of Rick Swope and JoJo:* The story of Rick Swope and JoJo can be found in Jane Goodall, *Reason for Hope: A Spiritual Journey* (New York: Warner Books, 2000). See also: Jane Goodall, "Essays on Science and Society," *Science* 5397 (December 18, 1998): 2184–2185, http://www.sciencemag.org/cgi/content/full/282/5397/2184?ck=nck.

50 *three men near my hometown of Boulder:* This story appeared in the *Boulder Camera*, February 1, 2005.

50 *A recent study, looking at fear in humans:* P. Vuilleumier, "Staring Fear in the Face," *Nature* 433 (2005): 22–23.

51 *In December 2005 a fifty-foot fifty-ton female humpback whale:* Peter Fimrite, "Daring Rescue of Whale off Farallones," *San Francisco Chronicle*, December 14, 2005, http://www.sfgate.com/cgi-bin/article.cgi?f=/c/a/2005/12/14/MNGNKG7Q0V1.DTL.

52 *the whale probably swam in circles:* Anita Bartholomew, "Whale of a Rescue," *Reader's Digest*, May 2006, http://www.rd.com/content/openContent.do?contentId=26512.

53 *"the pursuit of enjoyment is a primary emotion in our lives...":* Daniel Goleman, *Destructive Emotions: A Scientific Dialogue with the Dalai Lama* (New York: Bantam, 2004): 200.

53 *One researcher tells of watching a female chimpanzee give birth:* Douglas Starr, "Animal Passions," *Psychology Today* (March/April 2006): 98.

54 *hens love to play, and they're smart, moody, emotional:* Rosamund Young, *The Secret Life of Cows* (Preston, UK: Farming Books and Videos Ltd. Preston, 2005).

54 *"For too long scientists have denied the existence...":* This quotation

and the one about fish crows can be found in Jonathan Balcombe, "Animal Pleasure," in *Encyclopedia of Animal Behavior*, ed. Marc Bekoff (Westport, CT: Greenwood Publishing Group, 2004): 563–565.

55 *"Sentient animals have the capacity to experience pleasure . . ."*: Jonathan Leake, "The Secret Life of Moody Cows," *The Sunday Times*, February 27, 2005, http://www.timesonline.co.uk/article/0,,2087-1502933,00.html.

56 *dopamine (and perhaps serotonin and norepinephrine) are important:* Steve Siviy, "Neurobiological Substrates of Play Behavior: Glimpses into the Structure and Function of Mammalian Playfulness," in *Animal Play: Evolutionary, Comparative, and Ecological Perspectives*, eds. Marc Bekoff and J. A. Byers (New York: Cambridge University Press, 1998): 221–242.

56 *"a breathy, pronounced, forced exhalation . . ."*: P. Gorner, "Animals Enjoy Good Laugh Too, Scientists Say," *Chicago Tribune*, April 1, 2005. See also: "Sounds of Dog's 'Laugh' Calms Other Pooches," *ABC News*, December 4, 2005, http://www.abcnews.go.com/GMA/Health/story?id=1370911.

56 *play panting during social play in wild chimpanzees:* Takahisha Matsusaka, "When Does Play Panting Occur During Social Play in Wild Chimpanzees?" *Primates* 45 (2004): 221–229.

57 *"Research on rough-housing play in mammals . . ."*: Jaak Panksepp, "Beyond a Joke: From Animal Laughter to Human Joy," *Science* 308 (2005): 62–63.

57 *"It's like the behavior of young children . . ."*: Robert Provine, *Laughter: A Scientific Investigation* (New York: Penguin Books, 2001).

61 *"As he gets closer, and the roar of the falling water gets louder . . ."*: Jane Goodall, "Primate Spirituality," in *The Encyclopedia of Religion and Nature*, ed. B. Taylor (New York: Thoemmes Continuum, 2005): 1303–1306.

62 *"Tragedy struck in 1997. Fourteen's mate, Thirteen . . ."*: Doug

Smith, "Meet Five, Nine, and Fourteen, Yellowstone's Heroine Wolves," *Wildlife Conservation* (February 2005): 32.

63 *these wonderful beasts of burden show concern:* Janet Baker-Carr, *An Extravagance of Donkeys* (iUniverse, Inc., 2006).

63 *Some scientists even say that the demeanor of elephants:* C. Siebert, "An Elephant Crackup?" *New York Times Magazine*, October 8, 2006, 42, http://www.nytimes.com/2006/10/08/magazine/08elephant.html?ex=1161748800&en=c09919d33b237459&ei=5070. See also: G. A. Bradshaw, A. N. Schore, J. L. Brown, J. Poole, and C. Moss, "Elephant Breakdown," *Nature* 433 (2005): 807.

65 *"He was howling and banging his chest..."*: Janet Spittler, "Gorilla Religiosus," the Martin Marty Center, University of Chicago, March 3, 2005, http://marty-center.uchicago.edu/sightings/archive_2005/0303.shtml.

65 *baboons rely on friendships to help them cope with stressful situations:* A. E. Engh et al., "Behavioural and Hormonal Responses to Predation in Female Chacma Baboons (*Papio hamadryas ursinus*)," *Proceedings of the Royal Society of London: Biological Sciences Series B: Biological Sciences*, 273 (2006): 707–712. See also: "Baboons in Mourning Seek Comfort among Friends," University of Pennsylvania, January 30, 2006, http://www.upenn.edu/pennnews/article.php?id=902.

66 *"They stood around Tina's carcass, touching it gently..."*: This quotation and the following one by Cynthia Moss are from Cynthia Moss, *Elephant Memories: Thirteen Years in the Life of an Elephant Family* (Chicago: University of Chicago Press, 2000).

67 *Iain Douglas-Hamilton and his colleagues have shown that elephants:* Iain Douglas-Hamilton, S. Bhalla, George Wittemyer, and F. Vollrath, "Behavioural Reactions of Elephants Towards a Dying and Deceased Matriarch," *Applied Animal Behaviour Science* 100 (2006): 87–102.

67 *a unique field experiment to study the concern that elephants show:* Karen McComb, L. Baker, and C. Moss, "African Elephants Show

High Levels of Interest in the Skulls and Ivory of Their Own Species," *Biology Letters (The Royal Society)* 2 (2006): 26–28. See also: John Pickrell, "Elephants Show Special Interest in Their Dead," *National Geographic News*, October 31, 2005, http://news.nationalgeographic.com/news/2005/10/1031_051031_elephantbones.html.

68 *"With other wild animals, I have experienced many deep…":* Louis Dorfman, "The Truth About Animal Emotions," Lois Dorfman.com http://louisdorfman.com/truth_emotions.php.

68 *Jim and Jamie Dutcher describe the grief and mourning in a wolf pack:* Jim and Jamie Dutcher, *Wolves at Our Door* (New York: Pocket Books, 2002).

71 *Male marmosets spend a good deal of time figuring out who to mate with:* "Monkey Love: Male Marmosets Think Highly of Sex," *Science News*, February 21, 2004, http://www.sciencenews.org/articles/20040221/fob5ref.asp. See also: C. F. Ferris, C.T. Snowdon et al. "Activation of Neural Pathways Associated with Sexual Arousal in Non-human Primates," *Journal of Magnetic Resonance Imaging* 19 (2004): 168–175.

71 *Bernd Würsig describes the courtship of southern right whales:* Bernd Würsig, "Leviathan Lust and Love," in *The Smile of a Dolphin: Remarkable Accounts of Animal Emotions*, ed. Marc Bekoff (New York: Random House/Discovery Books, 2000): 62–65.

72 *Researcher Lee Dugatkin observed what he calls "guppy love":* Lee Dugatkin, "Risking It All for Love," in *The Smile of a Dolphin: Remarkable Accounts of Animal Emotions*, ed. Marc Bekoff (New York: Random House/Discovery Books, 2000): 66–67.

72 *"All these data lead me to believe that animals big and little…":* Helen Fisher, *Why We Love: The Nature and Chemistry of Romantic Love*. (New York: Henry Holt, 2004): 47.

73 *Australian leeches, or bloodsuckers, have been shown to be devoted parents:* "Slimy Leeches Are Devoted Parents," *Daily Times*

(Pakistan), March 7, 2004, http://www.dailytimes.com.pk/default.asp?page=story_3-7-2004_pg9_6.

73 *One day Naomi saw a mother surface without her calf:* Naomi Rose, "Giving a Little Latitude," in *The Smile of a Dolphin: Remarkable Accounts of Animal Emotions*, ed. Marc Bekoff (New York: Random House/Discovery Books, 2000): 32.

73 *In late February of one year, Echo, the "beautiful matriarch":* Cynthia Moss, "A Passionate Devotion," in *The Smile of a Dolphin: Remarkable Accounts of Animal Emotions*, ed. Marc Bekoff (New York: Random House/Discovery Books, 2000): 134–137.

75 *A one-year-old hippopotamus, named Owen by his caretakers:* C. Hatkoff, *Owen & Mzee: The Story of a Remarkable Friendship* (New York: Scholastic Press, 2006). See also: "Odd Couple Make Friends in Kenya," *BBC News*, January 6, 2005, http://news.bbc.co.uk/2/hi/africa/4152447.stm.

76 *the story of two beautiful malamutes, Tika, and her longtime mate, Kobuk:* Anne Bekoff, "In Sickness and in Health," in *The Smile of a Dolphin: Remarkable Accounts of Animal Emotions*, ed. Marc Bekoff (New York: Random House/Discovery Books, 2000): 61–62.

77 *Fifi was a female chimpanzee who Jane knew:* Jane Goodall, "Pride Goeth Before a Fall," in *The Smile of a Dolphin: Remarkable Accounts of Animal Emotions*, ed. Marc Bekoff (New York: Random House/Discovery Books, 2000): 166–167.

77 *Harvard University psychologist Marc Hauser observed:* Marc Hauser, "If Monkeys Could Blush," in *The Smile of a Dolphin: Remarkable Accounts of Animal Emotions*, ed. Marc Bekoff (New York: Random House/Discovery Books, 2000): 200–201.

78 *Biologist Anne Dagg, who studied giraffes:* Anne Dagg, "Graceful Aggression," in *The Smile of a Dolphin: Remarkable Accounts of Animal Emotions*, ed. Marc Bekoff (New York: Random House/Discovery Books, 2000): 76–77.

78 *According to Roland Anderson, their pearly white skin turns red:* Roland Anderson, "Seeing Red," in *The Smile of a Dolphin: Remarkable Accounts of Animal Emotions*, ed. Marc Bekoff (New York: Random House/Discovery Books, 2000): 84–87.

79 *Irene Pepperberg studied Alex, an extremely smart gray parrot:* Irene Pepperberg, "Ruffled Feathers," in *The Smile of a Dolphin: Remarkable Accounts of Animal Emotions*, ed. Marc Bekoff (New York: Random House/Discovery Books, 2000): 108–109. For a discussion of the fascinating studies conducted on Alex's cognitive abilities, see Irene Pepperberg, *The Alex Studies* (Cambridge, MA: Harvard University Press, 1999).

79 *Birds are also well known for their sibling conflicts:* For information on sibling conflict, see Douglas Mock, *More Than Kin and Less Than Kind: The Evolution of Family Strife* (Cambridge, MA: Harvard University Press, 2004).

80 *Researchers Kay Holekamp and Laura Smale studied spotted hyenas in Kenya:* Kay Holekamp and Laura Smale, "A Hostile Homecoming," in *The Smile of a Dolphin: Remarkable Accounts of Animal Emotions*, ed. Marc Bekoff (New York: Random House/Discovery Books, 2000): 118–121.

80 *"he was confident, unflinching, and played dirty...":* Robert Sapolsky, *A Primate's Memoir* (New York: Touchstone Books, 2002): 234.

81 *in Saudi Arabia, a man hit and killed a baboon with his car:* "Revenge Attack by Stone-throwing Baboons," *Ananova*, December 9, 2000, http://www.cs.cmu.edu/afs/cs/academic/class/16741-s06/www/baboons09122000.pdf.

82 *the story of Franz, a young male chimpanzee who was kept in a lab:* Ron Schusterman, "Pitching a Fit," in *The Smile of a Dolphin: Remarkable Accounts of Animal Emotions*, ed. Marc Bekoff (New York: Random House/Discovery Books, 2000): 106–107.

82 *Simon Baron-Cohen has made great strides... and ethologist Niko*

Tinbergen: Simon Baron-Cohen, *Mindblindness: An Essay on Autism and Theory of Mind* (Cambridge, MA: MIT Press, 1995); and E. A. Tinbergen and N. Tinbergen, "Early Childhood Autism — An Ethological Approach," *Advances in Ethology* 10 (1972).

Chapter 4

Some of the material in this chapter relies on my books *Minding Animals* and *Animal Passions and Beastly Virtues,* and on my essay "Wild Justice and Fair Play," all of which are listed in the bibliography.

Some other general references on play, morality in animals, and the relationship between play and morality include the following essays and books: Marc Bekoff, "Social Play Behaviour, Cooperation, Fairness, Trust and the Evolution of Morality," *Journal of Consciousness Studies* 8, no. 2 (2001): 81–90; Marc Bekoff, "The Evolution of Animal Play, Emotions, and Social Morality: On Science, Theology, Spirituality, Personhood, and Love," *Zygon: Journal of Religion and Science* 36 (2001): 615–655; Marc Bekoff, "Virtuous Nature," *New Scientist* (July 13, 2002): 34–37; and Marc Bekoff, "Wild Justice, Cooperation, and Fair Play: Minding Manners, Being Nice, and Feeling Good," in *The Origins and Nature of Sociality*, eds. R. Sussman and A. Chapman (Chicago: Aldine, 2004): 53–79.

Other resources focusing on animal play include G. M. Burghardt, *The Genesis of Play*; R. Fagen, *Animal Play Behavior*; and T. G. Power, *Play and Exploration in Children and Animals*. An interesting study is C. M. Drea and L. G. Frank, "The Social Complexity of Spotted Hyenas," in *Animal Social Complexity: Intelligence, Culture, and Individualized Societies*, eds. F. de Waal and P. L. Tyack (Cambridge, MA: Harvard University Press, 2003): 121–148.

85 *"Those communities which included the greatest number...":* Charles

Darwin, *The Descent of Man and Selection in Relation to Sex* (New York: Random House, 1871/1936): 163.

86 *the well-known field biologist George Schaller:* George Schaller and G. R. Lowther, "The Relevance of Carnivore Behavior to the Study of Early Hominids," *Southwestern Journal of Anthropology* 25 (1969): 307–341.

95 *Norwegian dog trainer Turgid Rugaas refers to play signals as "calming signals":* Turgid Rugaas, *On Talking Terms with Dogs: Calming Signals* (Wenatchee, WA: Dogwise Publishing, 2005).

95 *Jaak Panksepp discovered a close association between opiates and play in rats:* For more, see Jaak Panksepp, *Affective Neuroscience* (New York: Oxford University Press, 1998); and Jaak Panksepp, "Beyond a Joke: From Animal Laugher to Human Joy," *Science* 308 (2005), 62–63.

95 *James Rilling and his colleagues have used functional Magnetic Resonance Imaging:* James Rilling et al., "A Neural Basis for Cooperation," *Neuron* 36 (2002): 395–405.

96 *Researchers have identified a "trust center":* B. D. King-Casas et al., "Getting to Know You: Reputation and Trust in a Two-Person Economic Exchange," *Science* 308 (2005): 78. See also: Matthew Herper, "Measuring Trust with a Brain Scan," *Forbes*, March 31, 2005, http://www.hnl.bcm.tmc.edu/cache/Forbes_com%20Measuring%20Trust%20With%20A%20Brain%20Scan.htm.

98 *juvenile chimpanzees will increase the use of signals:* Jessica Flack, L. A. Jeannotte, and F. de Waal, "Play Signaling and the Perception of Social Rules by Juvenile Chimpanzees (*Pan troglodytes*)," *Journal of Comparative Psychology* 118 (2004): 149–159.

99 *Red-necked wallabies, kangaroos of a kind, also engage in self-handicapping:* Duncan Watson and D. B. Croft, "Age-related Differences in Playfighting Strategies of Captive Male Red-necked Wallabies (*Macropus rufogriseus banksianus*)," *Ethology* 102 (1996): 336–346.

99 *Sergio Pellis discovered that sequences of rat play:* Sergio Pellis, "Keeping in Touch: Play Fighting and Social Knowledge," in *The Cognitive Animal: Empirical and Theoretical Perspectives on Animal Cognition*, eds. M. Bekoff, C. Allen, and G. M. Burghardt (Cambridge, MA: MIT Press, 2002): 421–427.

100 *Recent research on nonhuman primates has shown that punishment:* For more on this research, see the following: R. Sussman and P. A. Garber, "Rethinking Sociality: Cooperation and Aggression Among Primates," in *The Origins and Nature of Sociality*, eds. R. Sussman and A. Chapman (Chicago: Aldine, 2004): 161–191; and R. Sussman, P. A. Garber, and J Cheverud, "The Importance of Cooperation and Affiliation in the Evolution of Primate Sociality," *American Journal of Physical Anthropology* 128 (2005): 84–97.

101 *Alexandra Horowitz observed a dog she called Up-ears:* Alexandra Horowitz, "The Behaviors of Theories of Mind, and a Case Study of Dogs at Play" (PhD diss., University of California, San Diego, 2002).

103 *"They [animals] have the ingredients we use for morality...":* Frans de Waal, "Honor Among Beasts," *Time* (July 11, 2005): 54–56.

104 *"I believe that at the most fundamental level our nature is compassionate...":* His Holiness the Dalai Lama, "Understanding Our Fundamental Nature," in *Visions of Compassion: Western Scientists and Tibetan Buddhists Examine Human Nature*, eds. R. J. Davidson and A. Harrington (New York: Oxford University Press, 2002): 68.

105 *"We believe that most donkeys...":* Michael Tobias and Jane Morrison, *Donkey: The Mystique of Equus asinus* (Tulsa, OK: Council Oak Books, 2006): 42.

105 *when treated fairly, many people will voluntarily cooperate:* Ernst Fehr and S. Gächter, "Altruistic Punishment in Humans," *Nature* 415 (2002): 137–140; Ernst Fehr and B. Rockenbach, "Detrimental Effect of Sanctions on Human Altruism," *Nature* 422 (2003):

137–140; and K. Sigmund, E. Fehr, and M. A. Nowak, "The Economics of Fair Play," *Scientific American* 286 (2002): 83–87.

105 *infants as young as eighteen months of age will help people in need:* Felix Warneken and Michael Tomasello, "Altruistic Helping in Human Infants and Young Chimpanzees," *Science* 311 (2006): 1301.

106 *Primatologists Robert Sussman and Paul Garber report that for diurnal prosimians:* Robert Sussman and Paul Garber, "Rethinking Sociality: Cooperation and Aggression Among Primates," in *The Origins and Nature of Sociality*, eds. R. Sussman and A. Chapman (Chicago: Aldine, 2004): 161–191; and Robert Sussman, Paul Garber, and J. Cheverud, "The Importance of Cooperation and Affiliation in the Evolution of Primate Sociality," *American Journal of Physical Anthropology* 128 (2005): 84–97.

107 *Some ecologists take this even further:* B. Shouse, "Ecology: Conflict Over Cooperation," *Science* 299 (2003): 644–646.

108 *"Justice presumes a personal concern for others . . . ":* Robert Solomon, *A Passion for Justice: Emotions and the Origins of the Social Contract* (Lanham, MD: Rowman & Littlefield Publishers, Inc., 1995): 102.

108 *"Forgiveness has a biological foundation that extends throughout the animal kingdom . . . ":* David Sloan Wilson, *Darwin's Cathedral: Evolution, Religion, and the Nature of Society* (Chicago: University of Chicago Press, 2002): 195, 212.

Chapter 5

111 *"Sometimes I read about someone saying with great authority . . . ":* Claudia Dreifus, "A Conversation with Frans de Waal," *New York Times*, June 26, 2001, http://select.nytimes.com/gst/abstract.html?res=F40B14FA3B540C758EDDAF0894D9404482.

118 *His Holiness the Dalai Lama planned to present a paper about neurotheology:* The quotes in this story are all from B. Carey, "Scientists Bridle at Lecture Plan for Dalai Lama," *New York*

Times, October 19, 2005, http://www.nytimes.com/2005/10/19/national/19meditate.html?pagewanted=all.

122 *"It is possible, therefore, that your simple man..."*: William J. Long, *Brier-patch Philosophy by "Peter Rabbit"* (Boston and London: Ginn & Company, 1906): 26.

122 *"In the late 1990s two remarkable novels were published..."*: Hal Whitehead, *Sperm Whales: Social Evolution in the Oceans* (Chicago: University of Chicago Press, 2004): 370–371.

124 *Psychologist Gordon Burghardt notes that denying our own intuitions:* Gordon Burghardt, "Animal Awareness: Current Perceptions and Historical Perspective," *American Psychologist* 40 (1985): 905–919.

124 *Donald Hebb, who loved to collect numbers and do statistical analyses:* Donald Hebb, "Emotion in Man and Animal: An Analysis of the Intuitive Process of Recognition," *Psychological Review* 53 (1946): 88–106.

124 *Lorenz noted that human beings are attracted to certain characteristics*: Konrad Lorenz, "Ganzheit und Teil in der tierischen und menschlichen Gemeinschaft," 1950. Reprinted in *Studies in Animal and Human Behaviour*, vol. 2, ed. R. Martin (Cambridge, MA: Harvard University Press, 1971): 135.

124 *"Do I get grief for the fact that in communicating..."*: Douglas Cruickshank, "Robert Sapolsky," *Salon*, May 14, 2001, http://dir.salon.com/story/people/conv/2001/05/14/sapolsky/index.html?pn=2. See also: Robert Sapolsky, *A Primate's Memoir* (New York: Touchstone Books, 2002).

125 *"Yes, we are human and cannot avoid the language and knowledge..."*: Stephen J. Gould, "A Lover's Quarrel," in *The Smile of a Dolphin: Remarkable Accounts of Animal Emotions*, ed. Marc Bekoff (New York: Random House/Discovery Books, 2000): 13–17.

126 *the story of Ruby, a forty-three-year-old African elephant:* Patricia Ward Biederman, "Soft Heart Under Her Thick Skin?" *Los Angeles Times*, November 16, 2004; this article can be found in the archives at www.ethologicalethics.org.

127 *"Obviously the mahouts [elephant keepers] may have many beliefs about the elephants . . .":* Mary Midgley was quoted by *Animal Sentience* on its website on September 4, 2005; for the original, please check the website's archives at www.ciwf.org.uk/sentience/.

129 *"It took us several years to believe what we were seeing . . .":* Sandra Blakeslee, "Cells That Read Minds," *New York Times*, January 10, 2006, http://www.nytimes.com/2006/01/10/science/10mirr.html?pagewanted=print. See also V. Gallese, "Mirror Neurons, from Grasping to Language," *Consciousness Bulletin* (Fall 1998): 3–4.

129 *Gallese and the philosopher Alvin Goldman suggest that mirror neurons:* Vittorio Gallese and Alvin Goldman, "Mirror Neurons and the Simulation Theory of Mind-reading," *Trends in Cognitive Science* 2 (1998): 493–501.

129 *Laurie Carr and her colleagues discovered, by using neuroimaging:* Laurie Carr et al., "Neural Mechanisms of Empathy in Humans: A Relay from Neural Systems for Imitation to Limbic Areas," *Proceedings of the National Academy of Sciences* 100 (2003): 5497–5502.

129 *Chris and Uta Frith have also reported results of neural imaging studies:* Chris Frith and Uta Frith, "Interacting Minds — A Biological Basis," *Science* 286 (1999): 1692–1695.

130 *Hal Markowitz's research on captive Diana monkeys:* Hal Markowitz, *Behavioral Enrichment in the Zoo* (New York: Van Reinhold Company, 1982).

130 *scientists at the Max Planck Institute for Evolutionary Anthropology:* A. P. Melis, B. Hare, and M. Tomasello, "Chimpanzees Recruit the Best Collaborators," *Science* 311 (2006): 1297–1300. See also: Bob Holmes, "Chimpanzees Show Hints of Higher Human Traits," *New Scientist*, March 2, 2006, http://www.newscientist.com/channel/life/dn8797.html.

130 *Recent research by Andrea Heberlein and Ralph Adolphs shows:* Andrea Heberlein and Ralph Adolphs, "Impaired Spontaneous Anthropomorphizing Despite Intact Perception and Social

Knowledge." *Proceedings of the National Academy of Sciences* 101 (2004): 7487–7491.

Chapter 6

133 *"Ethics in our Western world has hitherto . . .":* Albert Schweitzer, *Memoirs of Childhood and Youth* (London: Allen and Unwin, 1924).

135 *naturalists who gave animals "personalities" were vilified as "nature fakers":* For more on this movement, see R. H. Lutts, *The Nature Fakers* (Golden, CO: Fulcrum Publishers, 1990); and R. K. Gould, *At Home in Nature: Modern Homesteading and Spiritual Practice in America* (Berkeley: University of California Press, 2005).

136 *a wounded world, as the ecologist Paul Ehrlich calls it:* Paul Ehrlich, *A World of Wounds: Ecologists and the Human Dilemma* (Oldendorf/Luhe, Germany: Ecology Institute, 1997).

136 *"The nature of science is that it never . . .":* John Webster, "Animal Sentience and Animal Welfare: What Is It to Them and What Is It to Us?" *Applied Animal Behaviour Science* 100 (2006): 1–3. See also: John Webster, *Animal Welfare: Limping Towards Eden* (Oxford, England: Blackwell Publishing, 2005).

136 *"Because uncertainty never disappears, decisions about the future . . .":* Henry Pollack, *Uncertain Science . . . Uncertain World* (New York: Cambridge University Press, 2003): 3.

138 *By one count, in 2001 American laboratories conducted research:* L. Carbone, *What Animals Want: Expertise and Advocacy in Laboratory Animal Welfare Policy* (New York: Oxford University Press, 2004).

139 *"We are amending the Animal Welfare Act (AWA) regulations . . .":* Department of Agriculture, "Animal Welfare, Definition of Animal," RIN0579-AB69, Federal Register, vol. 69, no. 108, June 4, 2004, http://a257.g.akamaitech.net/7/257/2422/06jun20041800/edocket.access.gpo.gov/2004/pdf/04-12693.pdf.

140 *the Animal Welfare Act legally allows chimpanzees:* For the complete text of the Animal Welfare Act, visit U.S. Department of Agriculture at http://www.nal.usda.gov/awic/legislat/usdaleg1.htm. For a critical appraisal of the Animal Welfare Act, see *AV Magazine*, summer 2006, http://www.aavs.org/publications02.html.

140 *it was suggested that an opaque barrier be used to separate mice:* Ishani Ganguli, "Mice Show Evidence of Empathy," *The Scientist*, June 30, 2006, http://www.the-scientist.com/news/display/23764/#23829. See also: D. J. Langford et al., "Social Modulation of Pain as Evidence for Empathy in Mice," *Science* 312 (2006): 1967–1970.

140 *"The observed changes of acoustical parameters during the surgical period . . . ":* B. Puppe, P. C. Schön, A. Tuchscherer, and G. Manteuffel, "Castration-induced Vocalisation in Domestic Piglets (*Sus scrofa*): Complex and Specific Alterations of the Vocal Quality," *Applied Animal Behaviour Science* 95 (2005): 67–78.

140 *University of Wisconsin professor attached electrodes directly to the skins of pigs:* This story of Taser research is from the Stop Animal Tests website, www.stopanimaltests.com/f-taser.asp.

141 *psychologist Harry Harlow's well-known maternal deprivation studies:* For a summary of Harry Harlow's research, see D. Blum, *Love at Goon Park: Harry Harlow and the Science of Affection* (New York: Perseus Publishing, 2002). See also: the Psi Cafe website at www.psy.pdx.edu/PsiCafe/KeyTheorists/Harlow.htm.

141 *the prestigious Diabetes Research Institute published a report:* Diabetes Research Institute, "Researchers Find Striking Difference Between Human and Animal Insulin-producing Islet Cells," February 2006, http://www.diabetesresearch.org/Newsroom/NewsReleases/DRI/HumanIsletStructure.htm.

141 *in an essay published in the* Journal of the American Medical Association*:* J. Lazarou, B. H. Pomeranz, and P. N. Corey, "Incidence

of Adverse Drug Reactions in Hospitalized Patients," *Journal of the American Medical Association* 279 (1998): 1205. The number 106,000 is thought to be low because adverse drug reactions are underreported, according to Dr. John Pippin of The Physicians Committee for Responsible Medicine (PCRM); see also www.AnimalExperimentFacts.info.

142 *unsubstantiated allegations that the Oregon Regional Primate Research Center:* The details of this story are based on personal communications between Matt Rossell and the author.

144 *Françoise Wemelsfelder notes that the term "boredom":* The quotes here are from Françoise Wemelsfelder, "Animal Boredom: Understanding the Tedium of Confined Lives," in *Mental Health and Well-Being in Animals*, ed. F. McMillan (Oxford, England: Blackwell Publishing, 2005): 79–93. See also http://www.psyeta.org/hia/vol8/wemelsfelder.html.

145 *Georgia Mason and her colleagues have shown that at least 10,000 captive wild animals:* G. Mason, R. Clubb, N. Latham, and S. Vickery, "Why and How Should We Use Environmental Enrichment to Tackle Stereotyped Behaviour?" *Applied Animal Behaviour Science* (forthcoming).

145 *In one Dutch scientific laboratory:* Françoise Wemelsfelder, "Animal Boredom: Understanding the Tedium of Confined Lives," in *Mental Health and Well-Being in Animals*, ed. F. McMillan (Oxford, England: Blackwell Publishing, 2005): 79–93. See also: www.psyeta.org/hia/vol8/wemelsfelder.html.

146 *Professor Charles Gross conducted a study of marmosets:* Y. Kozorovitskiy et al., "Experience Induces Structural and Biochemical Changes in the Adult Primate Brain," *Proceedings of the National Academy of Sciences* 102 (2005): 17478–17482. See also: "Bored Monkeys Make for Stupid Monkeys," *New Scientist*, November 19, 2005, http://www.newscientist.com/channel/being-human/brain/mg18825266.100.

147 *In one study done on living dolphins:* Dorian Houser et al.,

"Structural and Functional Imagining of Bottlenose Dolphin (*Tursiops truncatus*) Cranial Anatomy," *The Journal of Experimental Biology* 207: 3657–3665.

148 *James Rilling and his colleagues have used PET scans to study the neural response:* James Rilling, J. T. Winslow, and C. D. Kilts, "The Neural Correlates of Mate Competition in Dominant Male Rhesus Macaques," *Biological Psychiatry* 56 (2004): 363–375.

148 *In 1998 in the United States alone:* http://animalliberationfront.com/Pratical/Health/health.htm.

149 *several good exposés of factory farming and the meatpacking industry:* Discussions about factory farming can be found in books by Gail Eisner, Michael W. Fox, Peter Singer and Jim Mason, Michael Pollan, Karen Davis, Eric Marcus, Matthew Scully, and Jane Goodall, among others. Animals other than cattle, pigs, and chickens need also to be considered in discussions of sentience. For example, there is evidence that lobsters and fish feel fear and pain: see T. Corson, *The Secret Life of Lobsters* (New York: Harper Perennial, 2004); S. Yue, R. D. Moccia, and I. J. H. Duncan, "Investigating Fear in Domestic Rainbow Trout (*Oncorhynchus mykiss*), Using an Avoidance Learning Task," *Applied Animal Behaviour Science* 87 (2004): 343–354; and L. U. Sneddon, "The Evidence for Pain in Fish: The Use of Morphine as an Analgesic," *Applied Animal Behaviour Science* 83 (2003): 153–162.

149 *they find themselves in containers called "4-D bins,":* I. Newkirk, *Making Kind Choices: Everyday Ways to Enhance Your Life Through Earth- and Animal-Friendly Living* (New York: St. Martin's Griffin, 2005): 235.

150 *the European Union has pledged to phase out wire battery cages:* The information on battery cages is from the EggIndustry.com website, which can be found at www.eggindustry.com.

150 *In October 2006, Germany banned seal products:* http://www.upi.com/NewsTrack/view.php?StoryID=20061022-012258-9417r

150 *"As we talked of freedom and justice one day for all . . .":* Alice

Walker, *Living by the Word* (New York: Harcourt Brace Jovanovich Publishers, 1988): 8.

151 *According to Lucas Reijinders and Sam Soret, compared to soy production:* Lucas Reijinders and Sam Soret, "Quantification of the Environmental Impact of Different Dietary Protein Choices," *Journal of Clinical Nutrition* 78 (2003): 664S–668S.

151 *"A single dairy cow belches and farts* 114 *kilos of methane a year..."*: James Bartholomew, "Let's Ban All the Methane Machines," *Telegraph*, April 7, 2004, http://www.telegraph.co.uk/opinion/main.jhtml?xml=/opinion/2004/07/04/do0403.xml&sSheet=/opinion/2004/07/04/ixop.html.

152 *"Little to no systematic research has been conducted on the impact of visits to zoos..."*: AZA, Executive summary: Visitor Learning in Zoos and Aquariums, http://www.aza.org/ConEd/MIRP/.

152 *"Any zoo that sits around and tells you..."*: V. Croke, *The Modern Ark: The Story of Zoos: Past, Present, and Future* (New York: Scribner, 1997): 171.

153 *the National Research Board on Agriculture and Natural Resources released the results:* To see the full report, called "Animal Care and Management at the National Zoo: Interim Report," visit: www7.nationalacademies.org/ocga/briefings/Animal_Care_Managment_National_Zoo.asp.

155 *In June 2006 an elephant named Gita died in the Los Angeles Zoo:* Jeanne McDowell, "Are Zoos Killing Elephants?," *Time*, June 12, 2006, http://www.time.com/time/health/article/0,8599,1203076,00.html.

156 *And what about Maggie, an African elephant:* Sarah Kershaw, "A 9,000-Pound Fish Out of Water, Alone in Alaska," *Anchorage Journal*, January 9, 2005, http://www.savewildelephants.com/page/NYTimes010905.pdf. See also: Blake de Pastino, "Elephant Shuns Jumbo Treadmill," *National Geographic*, May 19, 2006, http://news.nationalgeographic.com/news/2006/05/060519_elephant.html, and http://www.friendsofmaggie.net/.

157 *I and my students studied coyotes living in Grand Teton National Park:* For a summary of my research on coyotes, see Marc Bekoff and M. C. Wells, "Social Behavior and Ecology of Coyotes," *Advances in the Study of Behavior* 16 (1986): 251–338.

158 *Louis Dorfman and Scott Coleman use what they call "emotional enrichment":* To find out more about emotional enrichment, visit Louis Dorfman's website at http://louisdorfman.com/truth_emotions.php.

159 *a zoo in the Netherlands that is thoughtfully tending:* "Dutch Plan Orangutan Web Dating," *BBC News*, August 15, 2006, http://www.news.bbc.co.uk/2/hi/europe/4794279.stm.

159 *Suma, a forty-five-year-old elephant in the Zagreb Zoo in Croatia:* "Mozart Can Ease Suma's Blues,". *Classical Music Lounge*, June 30, 2006, http://cmlounge.wordpress.com/2006/07/28/63/.

159 *"The Bronx Zoo, one of the oldest and most formidable zoos in the country":* Charles Siebert, "An Elephant Crackup?" *New York Times Magazine*, October 8, 2006, http://www.nytimes.com/2006/10/08/magazine/08elephant.html?ex=1161748800&en=c09919d33b237459&ei=5070. See also: G. A. Bradshaw et al., "Elephant Breakdown," *Nature* 433 (2005): 807.

160 *"We are part of a generation of shame...":* This quote by Jill Robinson is from a personal communication with the author.

161 *the Yellowstone to Yukon (Y2Y) conservation initiative:* For more information on the Yellowstone to Yukon Conservation Initiative, visit www.y2y.net/.

161 *Numerous wild animals are killed by federal agencies:* The source for the numbers of animals killed by the U.S. Fish and Wildlife Service comes from the Animal Protection Institute, http://www.bancrueltraps.com/b_pred_killchartFY04.php. For more general information on federal predator control programs, visit Sinapu at www.sinapu.org/index.htm, and the Humane Society of the United States, www.hsus.org/wildlife/issues_facing_wildlife/lethal_predator_control_courtesy_of_wildlife_services/.

161 *"Officials acknowledge that killing deer and elk . . . ":* "Colorado Quits Killing Elk, Deer to Contain Disease," *Casper Star Tribune*, April 2, 2006, http://www.casperstartribune.net/articles/2006/04/02/news/regional/5e3061a2180d38868725714100749d91.txt.

162 *wolf culls don't work, and his organization is trying to raise money:* "Is Killing Off Big, Bad Wolves the Best Way to Halt Attacks," *Globe and Mail*, April 6, 2006, http://www.theglobeandmail.com/servlet/story/RTGAM.20060406.wxwolves06/BNStory/National/home.

162 *Kim Murray Berger has also shown that government-subsidized predator control:* Kim Murray Berger, "Carnivore-Livestock Conflicts: Effects of Subsidized Predator Control and Economic Correlates on the Sheep Industry," *Conservation Biology* 20 (2006): 751–761.

163 solastalgia, *which was coined by British professor Glenn Albrecht:* For more on the term solastalgia, visit http://home.iprimus.com.au/tammie1/Solastalgia.html.

163 *Theologian Stephen Scharper resolves this contradiction:* Stephen Scharper, *Redeeming the Time* (New York: Theommes Continuum, 1997): 188.

163 *the British Farm Animal Welfare Council created the "Five Freedoms of Animal Welfare":* For more on the Five Freedoms, visit the website of the Farm Animal Welfare Council at www.fawc.org.uk/freedoms.htm.

163 *First they ignore you:* http://www.quotedb.com/quotes/2776.

166 *We must make kind and humane choices:* This is a point stressed by many people. For numerous easy ways to do this, see I. Newkirk, *Making Kind Choices: Everyday Ways to Enhance Your Life Through Earth- and Animal-Friendly Living* (New York: St. Martin's Griffin, 2005).

Bibliography

The books and journals listed here contain much information about animal behavior, cognition, emotions, and well-being. Detailed information about numerous topics in ethology, cognitive ethology, and human-animal interactions can be found in my *Encyclopedia of Animal Behavior* and my *Encyclopedia of Human-Animal Relationships: A Global Exploration of Our Connections with Animals*.

Alcock, J. *Animal Behavior: An Evolutionary Approach*. 8th ed. Sunderland, MA: Sinauer Associates, Inc., 2005.

Allen, C., and Marc Bekoff. *Species of Mind*. Cambridge, MA: MIT Press, 1997.

Appleby, M. C., J. A. Mench, and B. O. Hughes. *Poultry Behaviour and Welfare*. Cambridge, MA: CABI Publishing, 2004.

Archer, J. *The Nature of Grief: The Evolution and Psychology of Reactions to Loss*. New York: Routledge, 1999.

Balcombe, J. *The Use of Animals in Education: Problems, Alternatives, and Recommendations*. Washington, DC: Humane Society of the United States, 2000.

———. *Pleasurable Kingdom: Animals and the Nature of Feeling Good.* London: Macmillan, 2006.

Bateson, P. P. G. "Assessment of Pain in Animals." *Animal Behaviour* 42 (1991): 827–839.

Becker, Marty. *The Healing Power of Pets.* New York: Hyperion, 2002.

Bekoff, Marc. "The Communication of Play Intention: Are Play Signals Functional?" *Semiotica* 15 (1975): 231–239.

———. "Social Communication in Canids: Evidence for the Evolution of a Stereotyped Mammalian Display." *Science* 197 (1977): 1097–1099.

———. "Play Signals as Punctuation: The Structure of Social Play in Canids." *Behaviour* 132 (1995): 419–429.

———, ed. *Encyclopedia of Animal Rights and Animal Welfare.* Westport, CT: Greenwood Publishing Group, 1998.

———. "Animal Emotions: Exploring Passionate Natures." *BioScience* 50 (2000): 861–870.

———, ed. *The Smile of a Dolphin: Remarkable Accounts of Animal Emotions.* New York: Random House/Discovery Books, 2000.

———. *Strolling with Our Kin: Speaking for and Respecting Voiceless Animals.* New York: Lantern Books, 2000.

———. *Minding Animals: Awareness, Emotions, and Heart.* New York: Oxford University Press, 2002.

———, ed. *Encyclopedia of Animal Behavior.* Westport, CT: Greenwood Publishing Group, 2004.

———. "Wild Justice and Fair Play: Cooperation, Forgiveness, and Morality in Animals." *Biology & Philosophy* 19 (2004): 489–520.

———. "Animal Emotions and Animal Sentience and Why They Matter: Blending 'Science Sense' with Common Sense, Compassion and Heart." In *Animals, Ethics, and Trade*, edited by J. Turner and J. D'Silva, 27–40. London: Earthscan Publishing, 2006.

———. "Animal Passions and Beastly Virtues: Cognitive Ethology as the Unifying Science for Understanding the Subjective, Emotional, Empathic, and Moral Lives of Animals." *Zygon: Journal of Religion and Science* 41 (2006): 71–104.

———. *Animal Passions and Beastly Virtues: Reflections on Redecorating Nature*. Philadelphia: Temple University Press, 2006.

———. "The Public Lives of Animals: A Troubled Scientist, Pissy Baboons, Angry Elephants, and Happy Hounds." *Journal of Consciousness Studies* 13 (2006): 115–131.

———, ed. *Encyclopedia of Human-Animal Relationships: A Global Exploration of Our Connections with Animals*. Westport, CT: Greenwood Publishing Group, 2007.

Bekoff, Marc, and C. Allen, "Cognitive Ethology: Slayers, Skeptics, and Proponents." In *Anthropomorphism, Anecdote, and Animals*, edited by R. W. Mitchell, N. Thompson, and L. Miles, 313–334. Albany, NY: SUNY Press, 1997.

Bekoff, Marc, C. Allen, and G. M. Burghardt, eds. *The Cognitive Animal: Empirical and Theoretical Perspectives on Animal Cognition*. Cambridge, MA: MIT Press, 2002.

Bekoff, Marc, and J. A. Byers, eds. *Animal Play: Evolutionary, Comparative, and Ecological Perspectives*. New York: Cambridge University Press, 1998.

Bekoff, Marc, and D. Jamieson. "Reflective Ethology, Applied Philosophy, and the Moral Status of Animals." *Perspectives in Ethology* 9 (1991): 1–47.

———. "Ethics and the Study of Carnivores: Doing Science While Respecting Animals." In *Carnivore Behavior, Ecology, and Evolution*, edited by J. Gittleman, 16–45. Ithaca, NY: Cornell University Press. 1996.

———, eds. *Readings in Animal Cognition*. Cambridge, MA: MIT Press, 1996.

Bekoff, Marc, and J. Nystrom. "The Other Side of Silence: Rachel Carson's Views of Animals." *Zygon: Journal of Religion and Science* 39 (2004): 861–883.

Berry, T. *The Great Work: Our Way Into the Future*. New York: Bell Tower, 1999.

Burghardt, G. M. "Amending Tinbergen: A Fifth Aim for Ethology." In *Anthropomorphism, Anecdote, and Animals*, edited by R. W. Mitchell, N. Thompson, and L. Miles, 254–276. Albany, NY: SUNY Press, 1997.

———. *The Genesis of Play*. Cambridge, MA: MIT Press, 2005.

Carbone, L. *What Animals Want: Expertise and Advocacy in Laboratory Animal Welfare Policy*. New York: Oxford University Press, 2004.

Cheney, D. L., and R. M. Seyfarth. *How Monkeys See the World: Inside the Mind of Another Species*. Chicago: University of Chicago Press, 1990.

Damasio, Antonio. *The Feeling of What Happens: Body and Emotion in the Making of Consciousness*. New York: Harcourt Brace, 1999.

———. *Descartes' Error: Emotion, Reason, and the Human Brain*. New York: Penguin, 2005.

Darwin, Charles. *The Descent of Man and Selection in Relation to Sex*. New York: Random House, 1871/1936.

———. *The Expression of the Emotions in Man and Animals*, 3rd ed. New York: Oxford University Press, 1872/1998.

Davis, K. *The Holocaust and the Henmaid's Tale: A Case for Comparing Atrocities*. New York: Lantern Books, 2005.

Dawkins, M. S. *Through Our Eyes Only?* New York: Oxford University Press, 1992.

de Waal, Frans. *Good-Natured: The Origins of Right and Wrong in Humans and Other Animals*. Cambridge, MA: Harvard University Press, 1996.

———. *Our Inner Ape*. New York: Riverhead, 2005.

———. *Primates and Philosophers: How Morality Evolved*. Princeton, NJ: Princeton University Press, 2006.

Dodman, Nicholas. *The Cat Who Cried for Help: Attitudes, Emotions, and the Psychology of Cats*. New York: Bantam, 1999.

———. *If Only They Could Speak: Stories About Pets and Their People*. New York: W. W. Norton & Company, 2002.

Drickamer, L. C., S. H. Vessey, and D. Meikle. *Animal Behavior: Mechanisms, Ecology, and Evolution*. Dubuque, IA: William C. Brown Publishers, 2001.

Dugatkin, L. A. *Principles of Animal Behavior*. New York: W. W. Norton & Company, 2003.

Dugatkin, L. A., and Marc Bekoff. "Play and the Evolution of Fairness: A Game Theory Model." *Behavioural Processes* 60 (2003): 209–214.

Duncan, I. J. H. "Poultry Welfare: Science or Subjectivity?" *British Poultry Science* 43 (2002): 643–652.

Dutcher, Jim, and Jamie Dutcher. *Wolves at Our Door*. New York: Pocket Books, 2002.

Eibl-Eibesfeldt, I. *Ethology*. New York: Holt, Rinehart, & Winston, 1975.

Eisner, G. A. *Slaughterhouse*. New York: Prometheus, 1997.

Fagen, R. *Animal Play Behavior*. New York: Oxford University Press, 1981.

Flack, J. C., and Frans de Waal. "Any Animal Whatever: Darwinian Building Blocks of Morality in Monkeys and Apes." *Journal of Consciousness Studies* 7 (2000): 1–29.

Fox, M. W. *Behaviour of Wolves, Dogs and Related Canids*. London: Jonathan Cape, 1971.

———. *Eating with Conscience*. Troutdale, OR: New Sage Press, 1997.

———. *Bringing Life to Ethics: Global Bioethics for a Humane Society*. Albany, NY: SUNY Press, 2001.

Fradkin, Philip. *A River No More*. Berkeley: University of California Press, 1996.

Francione, G. L. *Introduction to Animal Rights: Your Child or the Dog?* Philadelphia: Temple University Press, 2000.

Goodall, Jane. *Through a Window*. Boston: Houghton-Mifflin, 1990.

Goodall, Jane, and Marc Bekoff. *The Ten Trusts: What We Must Do to Care for the Animals We Love*. San Francisco: HarperCollins, 2002.

Goodall, Jane, with G. McAvoy and G. Hudson. *Harvest for Hope: A Guide to Mindful Eating*. New York: Warner Books, 2005.

Greek, C. R., and J. S. Greek. *Sacred Cows and Golden Geese: The Human Cost of Experiments on Animals*. New York: Theommes Continuum, 2000.

Griffin, Donald R. *The Question of Animal Awareness: Evolutionary Continuity of Mental Experience*. New York: Rockefeller University Press, 1976/1981.

———. *Animal Minds*. Chicago: University of Chicago Press, 1992.

Hauser, M. *Wild Minds*. New York: Henry Holt, 1999.

Heinrich, B. *Mind of the Raven: Investigations and Adventures with Wolf-Birds*. New York: Cliff Street Books, 1999.

Hinde, R. A. *Why Good Is Good: The Sources of Morality*. New York: Routledge, 2002.

Huffman, M. A. "Current Evidence for Self-Medication in Primates: A Multidisciplinary Perspective." *Yearbook of Physical Anthropology* 40 (1997): 171–200.

———. "Self-medicative Behavior in the African Great Apes: An Evolutionary Perspective into the Origins of Human Traditional Medicine." *BioScience* 51 (2001): 651–661.

Irvine, L. *If You Tame Me: Understanding Our Connections with Animals*. Philadelphia: Temple University Press, 2004.

Jordan, W. *A Cat Named Darwin: Embracing the Bond Between Man and Pet*. Boston: Mariner Books, 2003.

Kropotkin, P. *Mutual Aid: A Factor of Evolution*. Boston: Expanding Horizons Press, 1914.

Lehner, P. N. *Handbook of Ethological Methods*. New York: Cambridge University Press, 1996.

Levinson, Boris. *Pet-oriented Child Psychotherapy*. Springfield, IL: Charles C. Thomas, 1969.

———. *Pets and Human Development*. Springfield, IL: Charles C. Thomas, 1972.

Leyhausen, Paul. *Cat Behavior: The Predatory and Social Behavior of Domestic and Wild Cats*. New York: Garland, 1978.

Long, W. J. *Brier-patch Philosophy by "Peter Rabbit."* Boston and London: Ginn & Company, 1906.

Lorenz, Konrad Z. *Here I Am — Where Are You?* New York: Harcourt Brace Jovanovich, 1991.

MacLean, Paul. *The Triune Brain in Evolution: Role in Paleocerebral Functions*. New York: Plenum, 1970.

Marcus, E. *Meat Market: Animals, Ethics, and Money*. Newfield, NY: Brio Press, 2005.

Masson, J. *The Nine Emotional Lives of Cats: A Journey into the Feline Heart*. New York: Ballantine Books, 2004.

Masson, J., and S. McCarthy. *When Elephants Weep: The Emotional Lives of Animals*. New York: Delacorte Press, 1995.

Matsuzawa, T., ed. *Primate Origins of Human Cognition and Behavior*. New York: Springer, 2001.

McCarthy, S. *Becoming a Tiger: How Baby Animals Learn to Live in the Wild*. New York: Harper Perennial, 2005.

McMillan, F. D., with Kathryn Lance. *Unlocking the Animal Mind: How Your Pet's Feelings Hold the Key to His Health and Happiness*. Emmaus, PA: Rodale, 2004.

Midkiff, K. *The Meat You Eat*. New York: St. Martin's Griffin, 2004.

Mock, D. W., and G. A. Parker. *The Evolution of Sibling Rivalry*. New York: Oxford University Press, 1997.

Moss, C. *Elephant Memories: Thirteen Years in the Life of an Elephant Family*. Chicago: University of Chicago Press, 2000.

Newkirk, I. *Making Kind Choices: Everyday Ways to Enhance Your Life Through Earth- and Animal-Friendly Living*. New York: St. Martin's Griffin, 2005.

Panksepp, Jaak. *Affective Neuroscience*. New York: Oxford University Press, 1998.

———. "Affective Consciousness: Core Emotional Feelings in Animals and Humans." *Consciousness and Cognition* 14 (2005): 30–80.

Peterson, D. *Eating Apes*. Berkeley: University of California Press, 2003.

Pollan, M. *The Omnivore's Dilemma*. New York: Penguin Press, 2006.

Poole, Joyce. *Coming of Age with Elephants: A Memoir*. New York: Hyperion, 1996.

Power, T. G. *Play and Exploration in Children and Animals*. Mahwah, NJ: Lawrence Erlbaum Associates, Publishers, 2000.

Preston, S. D., and Frans de Waal. "Empathy: Its Ultimate and Proximate Bases." *Behavioral and Brain Sciences* 25 (2002): 1–72.

Rachels, James. *Created from Animals: The Moral Implications of Darwinism*. New York: Oxford University Press, 1999.

Regan, T. *The Case for Animal Rights*. Berkeley: University of California Press, 1983.

———. *Empty Cages: Facing the Challenge of Animal Rights*. New York: Rowman & Littlefield, 2005.

Ridley, M. *The Origins of Virtue: Human Instincts and the Evolution of Cooperation*. New York: Viking, 1996.

Rivera, Michelle. *Hospice Hounds*. New York: Lantern Books, 2001.

Rollin, B. E. *The Unheeded Cry: Animal Consciousness, Animal Pain, and Science*. New York: Oxford University Press, 1989.

Rothenberg, D. *Why Birds Sing: A Journey Through the Mystery of Birdsong*. New York: Basic Books, 2005.

Russell, W. M. S., and R. L. Burch. *The Principles of Humane Experimental Technique*. New York: Hyperion Books, 1959/1999.

Schoen, Allen. *Kindred Spirits: How the Remarkable Bond Between Humans & Animals Can Change the Way We Live*. New York: Broadway Books, 2001.

Scully, M. *Dominion: The Power of Man, the Suffering of Animals*. New York: St. Martin's Press, 2002.

Shapiro, Kenneth J. *Animal Models of Human Psychology: Critique of Science, Ethics, and Policy*. Seattle: Hogrefe and Huber, 1998.

Sharpe, Lynne. *Creatures Like Us?* Exeter, UK : Imprint Academic, 2005.

Singer, P. *Animal Liberation*, 2nd ed. New York: New York Review of Books, 1990.

Singer, P., and J. Mason. *The Way We Eat: Why Our Food Choices Matter*. Emmaus, PA: Rodale, 2006.

Skutch, A. *The Minds of Birds*. College Station, TX: Texas A&M University Press, 1996.

Sneddon, L. U. "The Evidence for Pain in Fish: The Use of Morphine as an Analgesic." *Applied Animal Behaviour Science* 83 (2003): 153–162.

Sober, E., and D. S. Wilson. *Unto Others: The Evolution and Psychology of Unselfish Behavior*. Cambridge, MA: Harvard University Press, 1998.

Solisti, K., and M. Tobias, eds. *Kinship with Animals*. Tulsa, OK: Council Oaks Books, 2006.

Tinbergen N. *The Study of Instinct*. New York: Oxford University Press, 1951/1989.

———. *The Herring Gull's World*. New York: Anchor Books, 1967.

———. *Curious Naturalists*. Amherst, MA: University of Massachusetts Press, 1984.

Turner, J., and J. D'Silva, eds. *Animals, Ethics, and Trade*. London: EarthScan Publishing, 2006.

von Frisch, K. *The Dance Language and Orientation of Bees*. Cambridge, MA: Harvard University Press, 1993.

Waldau, P., and K. Patton, eds. *A Communion of Subjects: Animals in Religion, Science, and Ethics*. New York: Columbia University Press, 2006.

Walton, Stuart. *A Natural History of Human Emotions*. New York: Grove Press, 2006.

Webster, J. *Animal Welfare: Limping Towards Eden*. Oxford, UK: Blackwell Publishing, 2005.
Weil, Z. *Above All, Be Kind: Raising a Humane Child in Challenging Times*. British Columbia, Canada: New Society Publishers, 2003.
Wilson, David Sloan. *Darwin's Cathedral: Evolution, Religion, and the Nature of Society*. Chicago: University of Chicago Press, 2002.

Index

Page numbers in *italics* refer to illustrations.

About the Author

Marc Bekoff is professor emeritus of biology at the University of Colorado–Boulder, a fellow of the Animal Behavior Society, and a former Guggenheim Fellow. In 2000 he was awarded the Exemplar Award from the Animal Behavior Society for major long-term contributions to the field of animal behavior. Marc is also a regional coordinator for Jane Goodall's Roots & Shoots program and a member of the Ethics Committee of the Jane Goodall Institute. In 2000 he and Goodall cofounded the organization Ethologists for the Ethical Treatment of Animals/Citizens for Responsible Animal Behavior Studies (www.ethologicalethics.org). Marc is on the board of directors of the Fauna Sanctuary, the Cougar Fund, and the Skyline Sanctuary and Education Center. He serves on the advisory board for Animal Defenders, the Laboratory Primate Advocacy Group, and the conservation organization SINAPU. He is an honorary board member of Rational Animal, Animalisti Italiani, and Fundacion Altarriba. He also has been part of the international program Science and the Spiritual Quest II and the American Association for the Advancement of Science (AAAS) Dialogue on Science, Ethics, and Religion. In 2005 Marc was presented with the Bank One Faculty Community Service Award for the work he has done with children, senior citizens, and prisoners.

Marc's main areas of research include animal behavior, cognitive ethology (the study of animal minds), and behavioral ecology, and he has also written extensively on animal protection. He has published more than two hundred papers and numerous books. His work has been featured in such publications as *Time* magazine, *Life* magazine, *U.S. News and World Report*, the *New York Times*, *New Scientist*, *BBC Wildlife*, *Orion*, *Scientific American*, *Ranger Rick*, and *National Geographic Kids*; on the CNN, NPR, BBC, and Fox networks; and on the programs *Good Morning America*, *Nature*, *48 Hours*, *GEO Natur*, the Discovery Channel's *Why Dogs Smile and Chimpanzees Cry*, Animal Planet's *The Power of Play*, and National Geographic Society's *Hunting in America* and *Play: The Nature of the Game*.

Marc's hobbies include cycling, skiing, hiking, and reading spy novels. In 1986 Marc became the first American to win his age-class at the Tour du Var bicycle race (also called the Master's/age-graded Tour de France). He lives outside of Boulder, Colorado. His website is http://literati.net/Bekoff/.

NEW WORLD LIBRARY is dedicated to publishing books and other media that inspire and challenge us to improve the quality of our lives and the world.

We are a socially and environmentally aware company, and we strive to embody the ideals presented in our publications. We recognize that we have an ethical responsibility to our customers, our staff members, and our planet.

We serve our customers by creating the finest publications possible on personal growth, creativity, spirituality, wellness, and other areas of emerging importance. We serve New World Library employees with generous benefits, significant profit sharing, and constant encouragement to pursue their most expansive dreams.

As a member of the Green Press Initiative, we print an increasing number of books with soy-based ink on 100 percent postconsumer-waste recycled paper. Also, we power our offices with solar energy and contribute to nonprofit organizations working to make the world a better place for us all.

Our products are available
in bookstores everywhere.
For our catalog, please contact:

New World Library
14 Pamaron Way
Novato, California 94949

Phone: 415-884-2100 or 800-972-6657
Catalog requests: Ext. 50
Orders: Ext. 52
Fax: 415-884-2199
Email: escort@newworldlibrary.com

To subscribe to our electronic newsletter, visit
www.newworldlibrary.com